A MESSAGE FROM HEAVEN

For Nancy & Gerry

Acknowledgements

I have been following the story of Fr Sean Fortune for a number of years and during that time received help from so many people. A number of them are named in the book while others prefer to remain anonymous. I am grateful to them all. This was not the easiest of subjects to tackle, but the flip side of that has been the people that I met during the course of my research. They showed amazing spirit and generosity, often overcoming painful experiences to speak about it because they wanted this story to be told. Without them there would be no book.

Four years is a long time for any newspaper to wait for a reporter to produce a story. The protracted legal process surrounding this case meant it was not possible for *The Irish Times* to print anything during this time; yet there was never a murmur when I said I needed to make another trip to Wexford, nor later when I needed time to write this book.

Finally I would like to thank my friends and family for their advice, encouragement and support.

ALISON O'CONNOR

A MESSAGE FROM HEAVEN

The Life and Crimes of
Father Sean Fortune

First published in 2000 by
Brandon
an imprint of Mount Eagle Publications
Dingle, Co. Kerry, Ireland

10 9 8 7 6 5 4 3 2 1

ISBN 0 86322 270 6
(original paperback)

Cover design by id communications, Tralee
Typeset by Red Barn Publishing, Skibbereen
Printed by ColourBooks Ltd, Dublin

Contents

Chapter 1

"We Will Always Be His Alleged Victims"

F<small>R</small> S<small>EAN</small> F<small>ORTUNE</small> died as he had lived. Dramatically. Alone in the bedroom of his small house, he assembled the instruments of his suicide: packets and vials of pills and a bottle of whiskey to wash them down. A TV screen in the corner of the room, linked to an outside security camera, relayed images of a cold March night in New Ross, County Wexford. Steel security shutters on the windows and doors transformed the terraced house into a mini-fortress. A sign on the wall warned passers-by that they were being recorded. That night, behind the shutters, Sean Fortune was succumbing to the effects of the lethal concoction. Still wearing his priestly garb, his glasses perched on his nose, he lay down on the bed. Wrapping rosary beads in his hands, he drifted into unconsciousness. At the age of forty-five he had taken his own life.

He had prepared well for the moment. On the dressing table was a poem which he had titled "A Message from Heaven to my Family". At the top of the page a hand-written note read: "From Father John Fortune. Please read out at my Requiem in Ballymurn." Beside the poem a sealed envelope, addressed to his brother, contained his will. Near by was his prayer book. It would be over thirty-six hours before he would be discovered. He had planned it that way.

Around 9pm that Thursday night he had telephoned

Margaret Stamp, who had been his housekeeper for fourteen years. "Don't bother coming in tomorrow," he told her, explaining that he was going away for the day with a priest friend. She offered to come anyway and collect the post. "Don't bother," he replied, "I'm going to be away." Before the conversation ended, she reminded him to open the security shutters on the door before she arrived on Saturday morning.

Later that night, around midnight, the telephone rang in the home of Peter Bennett, who did odd jobs and who had looked after the priest's house in New Ross for three years. Peter was annoyed to be disturbed at that late hour, particularly since the telephone stopped ringing just as he reached it. An hour later it rang again. This time the automated Eircom voice told him that a new message had been received in his voice mailbox. Peter was surprised to hear it was Fr Fortune, telling him not to come in the following day: "I'll be away," he said.

Earlier that day Peter and Margaret had both been in the house which the priest had called "Our Lady of Fatima Presbytery". "He seemed in good enough form," Peter recalled afterwards.

That afternoon Margaret had driven Fr Fortune to Waterford and on the way there they had talked about the weather and his health. He told her he was in a lot of pain, but he did not mention what he planned to do. The next day, despite knowing that he was going to be away, she thought it odd that he did not telephone "as he always did". She tried to call him a number of times but there was never a reply.

On Saturday she arrived at his house shortly after 11am, a little earlier than arranged. She saw that the shutters were locked and when she knocked there was no reply. Feeling there was something wrong, she immediately called Peter, who came straight from home. Peter had strict instructions about when he was allowed to enter the house because, as

Fr Fortune had told him, some important people came there for mass and to be healed. Emphasising the importance of their privacy, he said that Peter should only come in with his permission, but that morning Peter used his own keys to unlock and lift the shutters and he and Margaret went inside. The alarm was not activated and had not been set since Thursday. Peter thought it very strange because Fr Fortune always made sure to activate it when he was leaving the house.

"I knew at that stage something was wrong."

Walking into the kitchen, Peter remarked on a bad smell in the house. Fearful that something was amiss, Margaret raced up the stairs, with Peter following close behind. Opening Fr Fortune's bedroom door slightly, they saw him lying on the bed. When Peter turned on the light, it was obvious that he was dead. Looking around they saw the empty pill packets strewn about and what looked like powdered medication contained in an ordination chalice. A half litre bottle of Powers Gold Label whiskey lay upturned in a plastic bucket with tablets floating at the bottom in the spilled booze. The note to his family said that by the time they read it he would be with their parents in heaven and looking down on them. He could no longer stand what had been going on, he wrote. He was going to a better place. He wrote that he blamed the media for his misfortune, saying it had spread lies about him.

It was 11.55am when Margaret called a doctor, a priest and the gardaí. Five minutes later the gardaí were at the house. It was not a pleasant task for those assembled, but it took on a surreal edge when they entered downstairs and saw a makeshift church there, complete with altar, pulpit and anything else you might expect to find in a house of God. Going upstairs they saw that one of the bedrooms was laid out as a prayer room with seats arranged in a circle. In the bedroom they saw the priest and looked for a pulse but found none. Examining the scene, they quickly concluded that no foul play had been involved. A local doctor pronounced him dead and two local priests said prayers.

As word of the suicide spread quickly throughout New Ross and beyond, a crowd gathered outside to watch. Inside the house, undertakers struggled with the coffin containing the twenty-stone body. A door had to be removed from its hinges before they could carry it downstairs and outside to the waiting hearse. News of the death was conveyed to his family. Fr Fortune's sister had been expecting him to call as usual on the next day, a Sunday. The appointment was written into his diary. He had told his brother in Gorey that he would call in the afternoon with a Mother's Day cake for his sister-in-law. The cake was found in the boot of his car.

There were others who needed to be informed of his death. Chief among them were eight young men. Some lived in Wexford, others abroad. Over a period of years they had been sexually abused by Fr Sean Fortune. In a review of his life, the crimes against these young men would be his worst, but far from his only wrongdoing. Over decades an incredible number of complaints about his many exploits – sexual, financial and downright farcical – were logged against this man, both to his superiors in the Church and others in authority, but still he remained in a position of trust and, most importantly, power. Instead of ministering to his flock, he lied, cheated, bullied and abused. In the midst of it all he built up a public profile which made him one of the best known priests in the country. Attempts were made to bring him into line, but it is clear now that they did not work, and for many years it seemed as if nothing were being done. Former parishioners tell of how they they made specific, repeated and increasingly desperate complaints to the churchmen, chief among them the Bishop of Ferns, Dr Brendan Comiskey, but they felt little if no action was being taken and as if they were left to try and protect themselves and their children on their own. In so many sad and tragic cases they failed.

Even today the actions of this man, a Catholic priest, seem incredible. The bitter community divisions created by him are still deeply felt.

It was in February 1999 that the step was finally taken that would expose his misdeeds publicly. One of the many boys he abused, Colm O'Gorman, now a young man, summoned up the courage to make a complaint to the gardaí. Colm, originally from Wexford town, made a statement to the gardaí which began an investigation that would result in sixty-six charges of sexual abuse being brought against Fr Sean Fortune. Consistently he would deny the allegations. He was, he said, the victim of a conspiracy. For over four years he dragged out the legal process using different aspects of the law to avoid a trial.

But in March 1999, he must have realised that the day of reckoning could no longer be held off. A guilty verdict, jail sentence and public ignominy awaited. The man who had once loved the spotlight felt himself buckling under its glare. Eleven days before his death, he had stood in Wexford Circuit Court and listened as the charges against him were read out. Sitting behind him in the courtroom were the eight who said he had abused them, supported by their families. To each charge he had pleaded not guilty, but he must finally have known that the game was up.

His suicide, like any suicide, was shocking. There are some who believe that the decision to take his own life was "best for all", particularly his victims, because it would save them the pain of the trial. The reality is that it offered no comfort to any of those involved – not to his family, who have suffered greatly, and not to the gardaí, who devoted such time and effort to the investigation. For the man behind the investigation, Detective Garda Pat Mulcahy, it was an abrupt, frustrating and tragic end to years of hard work – just when a conclusion had seemed so close. Last but not least, it meant the eight young men were cheated of their opportunity to have their allegations of sexual abuse against Fortune tried in a court of law. They would never see a jury find him guilty of those crimes or have the opportunity to take the stand themselves and tell him, one after the other, what damage he had caused to their lives.

One of the young men, Don (not his real name), explains what the suicide of his abuser meant to him: "Everyone believes us, but in the eyes of the law we will always be his alleged victims. I will never be able to look him straight in the eye and say, 'You did this to us.' "

Chapter 2

Bingo

It WAS A win at bingo that finally brought running water into the home of the Fortune family in Gorey, County Wexford. Her children remember the Saturday night that their mother Elizabeth won £50; by Monday they had the everyday utility in the house. The Fortunes lived in Forest Cottage on the outskirts of the town. With six children in the family it was a struggle to survive. Jimmy Fortune, their father, originally from Kilanerin, north of the town, was a man well liked and respected. He is remembered for having a fine singing voice, and during the 1940s he was involved in local dramatic productions. His wife, Elizabeth Acton, grew up in the town and met her husband-to-be in the early 1950s. Jimmy was sixteen years older than his bride, who was in her twenties when they married.

The couple lived in a small, somewhat isolated cottage on the Courtown Road. John Joseph was their first child, born on 20 December 1953. Many years later, in London, Fr Fortune would tell Dr J.R.W. Christie Brown, a consultant psychiatrist, that he had been a healthy baby apart from a minor deformity affecting his toes, which was corrected by an operation when he was two years old. Five more children followed. Fr Fortune would tell the psychiatrist that it was a home with a happy atmosphere and a great emphasis on family life and religion. As the oldest child, he said, he was expected to show leadership.

Jimmy worked for many years as a forester before getting

a job as a gardener in the Loretto convent in nearby Arklow. He would cycle the eight miles there, returning home at weekends. He was not a familiar figure in local pubs. On Christmas Eve he would send some of the older children to the nearby Bridge Bar to buy a couple of bottles of Babycham. Elizabeth knitted her fingers bare to keep the children clothed.

Fr Fortune would describe his father as a gentle person, devoted to the family. In the dynamics of the family, he is remembered as the more shadowy figure in the background, while Elizabeth was the dominant one. Fortune said that she was a more outgoing person than his father, caring and involved in local community activities. She is the one that people remember.

As the children grew up and began to attend school, they were quiet and well behaved, never in trouble. Sometimes they seemed afraid of their mother, who was very highly strung and appeared unstable. People were wary of her because she would take issue with what she saw as any infringement of her rights. She was someone you moved around gingerly, careful of what you said to her. One Gorey man remembers his own mother telling of how she came across young John Fortune on the main street one morning as he stood whimpering at the door of a shop because he had been sent into town for sugar but the shop was closed. He did not want to return home without it.

Elizabeth suffered bouts of elation and then periods of depression. At times she could become very low in spirit. At different times she was hospitalised in St Senan's psychiatric hospital in Enniscorthy. Her children are protective of their memory of her. They remember the illness, when she had her bad days, but prefer not to think of her as erratic and difficult but as someone who did her best for her family, someone who had motivation and who got things done. They remember she had dreams and ambitions and she worked to get them. On the night that she won the £50 at bingo she decided immediately that it would pay to bring running water into the house.

In Gorey today there is much sympathy for this troubled family, and people are reluctant to speak about the circumstances of the Fortune family. There are a number of families of Actons, Elizabeth's relatives, living in the town. Loyalties are strong.

Her eldest son John would take after his mother in many ways. He attended national school at the local Loreto convent before moving to the Christian Brothers school. The family was proud of the eldest boy. He was a very good student, always near the top of the class.

Like his father, he liked drama and took part in local productions. As he grew older his interest in the Church grew and he served as an altar boy. Later, he would say that his own sexual abuse began when he was eight years old in Gorey and continued during his teenage years. He never identified the abusers. All he would say was that "some of the people were still living and others had gone to their maker". There is no way of ever knowing the truth of this now. Did he use it simply as a convenient explanation for his own behaviour? What is certainly true is that his family background would have made this young boy stand out as a child vulnerable to abuse.

As the 1960s came to an end, the Christian Brothers in the town spotted potential in young John. In July 1969 he left Gorey at the age of fifteen for the Christian Brothers juniorate in Carriglea Park in Dún Laoghaire, which he later said that he enjoyed. He claimed that during his four years at the juniorate he was senior student of his year each year. After that his family only saw him rarely, but they were happy for him and glad of the opportunity he had been given.

Less than a year after he left for the Dublin boarding school, his father, only fifty-six years old, died of a heart attack at the convent in Arklow. It was a huge blow to his wife. The family remember that the couple had a happy marriage and believe that at that time her spirit died with him. Afterwards Elizabeth's condition would deteriorate. It was difficult coping with the five children who remained at home.

The youngest child was only a toddler when his father died. The second eldest son took over the parental role, helping his mother with the younger children. John continued his schooling in Dublin, making very occasional visits home. He sat his Leaving Certificate in Mount St Mary's school in Bray and told people that with seven honours he could have studied medicine but decided to become a Christian Brother. Ten days after finishing his schooling, he entered the novitiate in St Helen's in Booterstown in County Dublin, in August 1973. However just over a month later he left, saying he wanted to be a priest. According to what he told Dr Christie Brown, the Christian Brothers were upset that he had decided to leave them, but he felt he was following his vocation.

Returning to Wexford he went to St Peter's seminary in the town. According to the Christian Brothers, their file on John Fortune contains nothing other than relevant dates. There is no record of any request from St Peter's seminary for a report on the young student who spent his teenage years with them but changed his mind about the nature of his vocation.

On 5 July 1976, three years after he entered the Wexford seminary, John's mother, who had become increasingly troubled, died at the age of forty-six. She had taken an overdose. According to the death certificate, the cause of Elizabeth Fortune's death was accidental. Her children are adamant that it was accidental and that this was established at the time. Her eldest son was twenty-two when his mother died. He would later say that her death had a devastating effect on him.

It had only been six years since the death of their father when the children had to bury their mother. Details of this period of the Fortune family history are sketchy. The second eldest son continued in his role as the family caretaker, looking after his sister and brothers. The baby of the family was just eight when he was orphaned. As time went on they looked at their eldest brother as one of the stronger members of the family. He was educated. He had direction. Without any backing, either financial or emotional, he had managed to get himself accepted to train for the priesthood, and when he was ordained they were very proud. They watched as he built up a public profile locally and nationally, featuring in newspaper articles, sometimes even writing them himself, and appearing on RTÉ programmes. They didn't see him often, but they knew from how he talked that he was very well thought of in Church circles.

In Gorey they also remember his progress from seminarian to priest and how he appeared to grow almost physically in stature, even taller than his six feet two inches, once he had a dog collar around his neck and the title "Father" before his name. You could even see it in the way he walked down the street, and if you stopped to talk to him much of the conversation was taken up with his boasting about his successes.

"We have a saying around here about people who would always have one better than you," explained a Gorey man who knew him. "He was like a cat with two willies."

Chapter 3

A Thin Line

IT WAS SHORTLY after his arrival as a seminarian in St Peter's College that John Fortune gained the nickname "Flapper". He was always in a hurry, flapping about the place. As a seminarian he is remembered as being somewhat eccentric, but always enthusiastic. Odd as he may have been, this young man's behaviour was not entirely outside the norm when compared with that of some others there at that time.

"An academy of debauchery." That is the strong description of St Peter's by Ger Walsh, a day pupil at the school in the 1970s. "It was bad enough before Fortune arrived and when he did things just got worse," says Walsh, now managing director of People Newspapers in Wexford. As well as being a seminary where young County Wexford men were trained to be priests, St Peter's was a school where the middle classes sent their sons to be educated, either as day pupils or as boarders.

Descriptions of the college at that time paint an almost surreal picture of a place where a handful of priests appeared to have a predilection for young boys, a few were gay, while some had girlfriends. Of course, there was a large number who behaved just as one would have expected of pious young men overseen by superiors who took their vocations very seriously. However, it appears that the young pupils who were there at the time witnessed some very unusual goings on.

A Thin Line

Looking back on his time as a student there in the 1970s, Don says it was a strange place. "Some of the seminarians were so camp they used to be running around the place like girls out of a Brontë novel. I don't remember any strong man wanting to be a priest, although there were the section who had girlfriends."

A priest familiar with St Peter's says that one of the problems was that it was a small seminary with ever dwindling numbers. In Maynooth, where he trained himself, there had been many hundreds of students. "It just was not a healthy, vigorous environment when you had so few fellas there."

Another priest who was a seminarian in St Peter's in the late 1960s says the regime became noticeably laxer in the 1970s because of the fall in numbers going for the priesthood. "The time we were there, you had to get permission to go down town to the dentist. But after that they seemed to go in the opposite direction, into a freefall, and threw discipline out the door. I couldn't believe the things I was hearing afterwards, about Fortune and all that. During my time, if you were found with a bar of chocolate you were likely to be thrown out. I remember one day Dean Paddy Curtis heard a transistor and he had the place pulled apart. We were all on bread and water for a month after it."

However, another man who was a seminarian there during that time maintains that it was run along military lines and there were strict rules. The seminarians, around eighty in number then, were treated more like children. "Everything was run by the book," he says. During their leisure time they played hurling and went to see plays. "None of the boys I hung around with had girlfriends. We just did the things you would expect, like going to cinemas and plays. What might go on in an inner circle you would not be privy to. The priest who was in charge kept a strict code of practice and ran a strict regime. It didn't matter if you were a senior or a junior, he looked on you the same. Most of the time in there we were studying and you would not have time for much else. Everyone hung around with their own group; a seminary is not a place where you hang around on your own," says the man, who left before ordination.

It's not known when Fortune began his career as an abuser, although it had certainly started by the time he reached St Peter's. However, he was certainly not the only priest there with a penchant for young boys. According to stories from other boys who attended the college, there was one priest whose pastime was standing around the corridors and "feeling up" the young boys as they went past. "He spent most of the time running up and down corridors and catching fellas by the arses," remembers one.

According to former pupils, Fortune quickly developed a reputation for himself, not least for his offer of a Mars bar each evening to the first-year boarder who would tell the dirtiest joke in the dormitory. Ger Walsh remembers being a student in his religion class around 1974.

"We had a very boring clerical student who took it all very seriously, but then the class was divided and half of us went into Flapper's class. We considered ourselves very fortunate. This was a time way before the Church introduced the notion that you could touch the host or drink the altar wine, but within no time he had us drinking the wine. He was practically saying mass in the class. There were only fourteen of us, and we didn't have great voices, but he used to have us singing like we were a black gospel choir. He would give us projects to do and would go mad if we did not take them very seriously. I remember when he formed the scout troop. I never heard any stories about him at that time being into boys; anyway we had enough to be doing trying to avoid the others."

Don's father Michael says that when he heard some of the rumours about what was going on at the time involving seminarians, he went to speak to the principal of the school, Fr John Gahan. Fr Pat Jordan, now dead, was also there.

"There were rumours going around which were bad for the school. I was concerned for my boys. Paddy Jordan said there was no possibility of anything like that going on there."

Canon Gahan, now based in Gorey, disputes this story. He has no recollection, he says, of any such complaints being made. "I am completely at sea. I have no recollection whatever of that. I can't remember ever having that meeting. The subject as far as I am concerned never came up. The whole thing came as a complete surprise later on."

Long-time Fortune watcher Billy Moroney from New Ross remembers the young clerical student spending summers in Duncannon, near Fethard-on-Sea on the Hook Peninsula in County Waterford. Fortune worked as a barman in the local hotel. While there he started a Scouts group and got local people involved. "Fortune was hyperactive. People liked him because he was always laughing and good humoured. I remember the local priest, Fr Cummins, was very elderly and he had a stroke. Fortune would be up on the altar, supposed to be helping him. He would be in front of him, behind him and beside him all at the one time, like a jack in the box. It's a wonder he didn't knock the poor man over. He used to try and preach the sermons as well. I remember they were like something a child would say on the altar. Some of it was just daft, and I understand that didn't change too much when he became a priest. You would look at him and think, 'That fella will never be ordained.' Some time after the Scouts were set up, there was some sort of a problem with money for uniforms. It was sorted out eventually, but afterwards when people found out more about him, they were saying that they bet it was Fortune."

Furthering his involvement in the Scouts Association, Fortune set up a group in St Peter's and became the scoutmaster. It was through this that the young seminarian became a close friend of Don's family, particularly his mother Brid, after he had started school there in 1977.

The enthusiastic young seminarian persuaded Brid to become involved in the Scouts group, along with a number of other parents.

Brid also remembers that parents involved in the Scouts group quickly found themselves pitted against each other. "He had this amazing gift of turning people against each other. I'm not easily manipulated, but I found myself doing things for him. I had children, a home, a busy husband – but he still managed to get me to change the flowers on the May altar every day for a month. He selected people to be on the Scouts Council, and they were all women. He had a way of making you feel special; it was not a sexual thing. I still don't know how he did it. I am usually fairly intuitive. He made you feel somehow privileged – that through him you were closer to God. He got us to collect his ordination suit from Clerys – that even felt like a privilege, driving through the traffic in Dublin. At one stage he told me that he was buying a car and he asked if Michael would go guarantor. He said he did not have the money. This was a signal to offer to pay, but I didn't. In the years after if we turned on the television and saw his pious face, it used to really annoy me."

Michael remembers Fortune as being somehow like a cult leader. "Women usually have marvellous intuition for everything; men are not as finely tuned. But Fortune did not fit the bill; he was not our own kind, if you know what I mean. Men had a feeling that he was just not kosher. He loved playing mind games and read an awful lot of psychology books."

One of the other parents involved in the Scouts group at that time was Lily Deasy from Wexford town. "When I look back now it is amazing how we were all so gullible. Someone else on the committee tipped me off about Fortune, saying that he had heard something about him and that I should keep an eye on the boys. I told him to tell the chairman, but he said he felt I was capable of doing what was needed. As we know now, that would have been some job. Someone else on the committee told me that our accounts had come up by £200, which was a lot of money at the time. I asked where did the money come from and I was told it was Fortune. The minute that man said it to me, I said: 'That came from a client,' and he told me that I was an awful woman for saying that. I used to stand up to Fortune. He set someone on me one day, tackling me about it, but I wasn't going to take that either."

One day Lily invited one of the other seminarians from St Peter's to her house. "I decided, 'This is my day.' I said to him that I was going to ask him something and that he better tell me the truth. My son would have been a senior scout, around fifth or sixth year at the time. 'Have you any information about yer man?' I asked. He told me that they had been over somewhere in the West of Ireland camping with Fortune when one of the boys went missing and a few of the others went off to look for him. While that was going on, Fortune imposed on one of the other boys, but the boy kicked out and he left him alone. The seminarian said that was all he knew. There was another seminarian from St Peter's that I told and he nearly died of shock. Of course, that made me even more alert with the kids. My son says that he knew what was going on with Fr Collins and Fortune, but he stayed away from them both, and luckily nothing ever happened to him."

That other priest to be avoided, Fr Donal Collins, had a reputation as a brilliant scholar, teaching physics in St Peter's. He was also involved in extra-curricular activities, making him popular with parents. For obvious reasons, the students nicknamed him "Paws". It appears that the sexual abuse he carried out during those years, although not the seriousness of it, was an open secret among students in the school. He had many opportunities for setting it up, especially in the swimming club which he ran. Of course, this was a role which brought with it the by-now-familiar "developmental checks" for the swimmers – an excuse for intimacy with his young charges. His other main area of interest was the Young Scientists Exhibition which involved bringing students to Dublin. In the 1980s Fr Collins would be appointed principal of St Peter's.

Ger Walsh believes that with the number of priests resident in the college at that time, it would have been next to impossible for some of them not to have noticed what was going on. "We knew about Collins and we knew, with a great degree of certainty, that Fortune was mad. There was no one in his class who would have told you any differently, and we were just teenagers. There was simply no control over him. I remember that one of the priests had a girlfriend, and he used to bring her up to his room. We felt that was a terrible thing at the time, but in fairness to him he left. To us the place seemed like an academy of debauchery. Since then a number of the priests have left and got married."

In his previous job as newspaper editor, Walsh would come across Fortune on a number of occasions in the years to come. "He was quite brilliant, but there is a thin line between brilliance and madness. He was at the other side of that line. He thought up some amazing schemes, and properly channelled he could have been brilliant as a government minister. He could really have shaken up an area."

Reflecting on the legacy of his schooldays, Walsh tells a poignant story of a recent reunion of his class in St Peter's College. Unusually for such an event, no priests were invited. Former classmates gathered and had a wonderful time reminiscing. Early in the evening they spent some time discussing Fortune and Collins and what had gone on. In hindsight there were many things which, sadly, now made sense to them. The classmates whose behaviour had changed so suddenly were those that had been abused. "I remember a boy who went from being top of the class to ending up in prison," says Walsh. Sadly they held a minute's silence for "absent friends".

A Thin Line

Don remembers that in Fortune's study in St Peter's there were psychology books with titles such as *Controlling Techniques in Dealing with Teenagers.* "He was a brilliant organiser and a masterful manipulator. He read an awful lot and took the stuff in books very literally. I remember when he wanted to start a football team and he stood in the middle of the field with a book in his hand, reading out to us and trying to demonstrate how you do the scissors kick. When he was finished he stood back and said, 'Now, you do it, lads.' There was a Scouts handbook where he had adapted well-known songs using his own words. I remember one of them in particular; we told him it was awful:

> I'm a Cub Scout,
> I'm a Cub Scout,
> I'm a Cub Scout
> Yes, I am
> And I'd rather be a Cub Scout
> Than a jar of jam.

Don laughs as he sings the familiar tune with the absurd lyrics, remembering the ridiculousness of it all.

"Being in charge, in control, was a big thing for him. Everyone in St Peter's College knew what he was up to. I guess it would have been seen as a 'better' school and maybe the kids were softer. The scouts were predominantly boarders. Their parents would travel up to fifty miles to a Scouts group meeting because he told them they had to. I remember in the Scouts a guy would suddenly leave, saying he didn't want to do it any more, and then he would be back a few days later and Johnny would tell us that he was now a patrol leader. I was a sensible kind of chap and he was strong at organising; he was always doing something. I suppose in my case I was impressed by him. But you know, when you are a kid you are put into situations that you do not like, but because you are a kid you have to put up with it. The thing about a con is that you know that you are being conned, shafted one way or another, but when you have no outside reference you don't know what to do. I was eleven when I went in to St Peter's and sixteen when I left. He fiddled with another lad in a tent in front of four or five of us on a Scout trip to Duncannon. I didn't realise what was going on at the time. I was probably a bit behind everyone else," he says wryly.

A priest who is acquainted with some of the seminarians who trained with Fortune says that they speak about three things they remember about him: "They say he was physically big and dominating. Secondly, he was an inveterate liar and thirdly, he could talk his way out of anything."

That priest wonders what report, if any, was given by the Christian Brothers when Fortune left them to go on to train as a priest in St Peter's or what report was forwarded from the seminary at the end of his training to Bishop Donal Herlihy, the then Bishop of Ferns.

"At the end there would have been a recommendation to ordain him. Very often if there was a question over someone they would have had to wait six months or a year, but Fortune went ahead on time. It amazes me how he got through the six years in the seminary."

Fortune himself would tell Dr Christie Brown that the only trouble he had had in the seminary was being reprimanded for making tea after night prayers. If he received any criticism, it was, he said, that he was inclined to take things too seriously.

Fortune was ordained on 27 May 1979. Don's parents remember the day well, particularly after having collected his suit. The photographs show a thin, sincere-looking young man wearing large square glasses. In one he has a smiling open face as he looks directly at the camera, clearly delighted to finally have made it. Brid and Michael remember that he acted strangely once the ceremony had concluded.

"As soon as he was ordained, he went in off the altar and fell down in tears. He did not come back for a long time.

Now I think maybe it was because of the doubts hanging over him. He knew he was lucky to have made it there," says Brid.

After ordination he was sent to Belfast for a year, where he was based at Holy Rosary Church, and would also visit Nazareth House orphanage in the south of the city. This was the same orphanage where the Norbertine priest Fr Brendan Smyth would abuse children when he was left alone with them in a room set aside for visitors. Years later Smyth had the dubious honour of becoming Ireland's most notorious paedophile priest as a result of an abusing career which spanned more than four decades, and he became the centre of an extraordinary political drama when his delayed extradition from the North to face charges resulted in the fall of the Fianna Fáil/Labour coalition in 1994.

It has been speculated that Smyth and Fortune crossed paths in Belfast; however, it is not known for sure whether the two priests came across each other or were friendly. Fortune's stay in the city was relatively short and it was around that time that Smyth was sent to North Dakota in the US where he served for three years.

Four months after Fortune's ordination, in September, Lily Deasy travelled from Wexford to attend the pope's mass in the Phoenix Park. There in the crowd she spotted Fortune, who had travelled down from Belfast.

"I nearly died when I saw him. He had all these little children with him. My instinct just cracked. I said, 'How can I stay in this place with this man?' There was a Wexford seminarian with me and I told him that as soon as we got back I was going to take it further. The seminarian did not believe what I told him about Fortune, but after a while he told me that he was after remembering that the gardaí had tried to contact him twice recently but that he had not gotten back to them. He just seemed to click that it might have been about Fortune. He told me not to do anything about it until he got back to me, so I didn't. I told a friend about it, but I said we could not do anything until we heard from the college.

"Then the seminarian asked me to come up to the college. I met him there and he told me it was true about Fortune and that was what the gardaí wanted to talk to him about. He said that he went to the bishop [Herlihy] and that it was being dealt with and that Fortune was going for treatment. I was happy but not for long, because then word came back from the North that he was up to the same thing again. When I asked my seminarian friend what was going to happen, he told me that they knew it for definite now and they were sending him a second time. In the years afterwards I thought he had been treated. I heard daft stuff about him, but I believed that was all he would have been up to and that was what his madness was being channelled into. I think now that the garda who was inquiring back then was Detective Seamus Quaid, who was killed in an IRA shooting in south Wexford around that time. I regret now that I did not do more. I was watching a snooker programme the other night and there was one of them on that looked just like him. I couldn't look at it. When I think of all the damage that he did to children. It was just terrible," says Lily.

Lily's fears about what he was doing in Belfast were very well founded. He wasted little time in picking his young prey – boys involved with the Scouts, those serving as altar boys and those in the orphanage. One of them, a twelve-year-old boy had been an altar boy at Holy Rosary Church and was also a scout. Fortune invited him to his home one night to discuss the Scouts. After a short time the priest suggested that they "play a game"; he started to tap the boy's penis and suggest that he do the same to him, then he began to fondle him. In his struggle to get away, the boy knocked them both to the floor from the couch, but the priest continued to hold him down. Eventually he got away and told Fortune that what he was doing was not right. He left the house threatening to tell the parish priest but in the end kept the incident to himself. He refused to continue as an altar boy, but about a month later he travelled to Gorey with a Scouts group that included Fortune. One afternoon he saw the priest standing between two younger scouts and Fortune was doing the same thing to them as he had done to him. He called the two young boys away from the priest, telling them that he had jobs for them to do. Once he got back to Belfast, he also packed in the Boy Scouts. Fortune left Belfast a short time later and he never saw him again.

After Belfast, Fortune's next stop was Dundalk where in 1981 he attended a course at the Institute of Religious Education at Mount Oliver. A local man who was a teenager at the time remembers the young priest well.

"He had the run of the schools in Dundalk," he recalls. "He used to hold these 'Youth Encounter' retreats. I remember he would have young married couples helping him, and they would tell us about how they had 'saved' themselves until their wedding night. He lived in a fancy, architect-designed, split-level house in the Cooley Mountains where he used to hold parties there and give out drink. I remember you got a sense off him, an iffyness. One day he came into the class and he had this wooden thing hanging around his neck. Someone asked him about it.

"'What's that, Father?'

"'A piece of the crucifix.'

"'The actual one?'

"'Yes it is,' he answered.

"'No way,' said yer man, but Fortune was insistent," says the Dundalk man, who now holds a high profile position but prefers to remain anonymous, along with the majority of those who took part in this book, all displaying a reluctance to being connected in any way with the priest.

During this time the young priest had kept in contact with Don's family. Their young boys were growing into teenagers and he was on hand to advise them on how to deal with this new stage in their children's development. Much to his delight, in the summer of 1981 Bishop Herlihy appointed him curate to Poulfur in Fethard-on-Sea in the south of Wexford. The proximity meant that he was able to visit the family more regularly. One day in April 1982, when the couple were abroad on holidays, he called to their home. An aunt and uncle were caring for the children. Fr Fortune came inside and chatted for a while to Don's younger brother Sean before going into the kitchen and asking if he could take Don for a short break to his home in Poulfur, which was just a forty-minute drive from Wexford. Don remembers the moment vividly and how he had been on the alert because of what he had witnessed Fortune doing to a boy on a camping trip, as well as other episodes. Instinctively he knew the moment the priest arrived at his home that he was in danger. Fortune had known that his parents were on holidays. He had planned it.

"Johnny was talking to my younger brother. I rushed in to my aunt and uncle, and I told them that he was going to ask to take me to his house and that they weren't to let me go. I said I couldn't tell them why, but that it was important. He told me he wanted me to come to Poulfur, that he had this new organ that he wanted me to see. I felt quite confident and told him that he would have to ask my aunt and uncle. But the smile was knocked off my face when I heard them tell him it was fine. I found myself heading off in the car with him. I don't blame them, they were brought up with the power of the Church. My auntie is the loveliest woman and she kills herself over it. We don't talk about it.

"I got into his car, knowing what was likely to happen. He had tried a few gropes before but I had pushed him away. There was a spare bedroom in the house and I assumed I would be sleeping there, but he insisted I sleep in his room that night. He was incredibly flattering, telling me, 'You're so funny, you're very perceptive, you're very intelligent. I think you are quite probably homosexual.' He was unrelentingly persistent. He just kept it up. At three or four o'clock in the morning, I was physically exhausted, but every time I started to drift he would be trying to make a move again. I remember he had a very strange body odour. I eventually fell asleep and when I woke up it was morning and he wasn't in the room. I went downstairs to the kitchen. He was there with the housekeeper. She gave me a look, which I felt seemed to say, 'another young boy'. There was something accusing in the way she looked at me, as if here I was, leading the priest astray. He dragged me around for two days down there. I have heard about all the telephones he was supposed to have had in the house but I couldn't find one in the place. In the car he would insist on holding my hands as we drove around to meet parishioners. I was as embarrassed as fuck. I kept saying I wanted to go home. I was exhausted from lack of sleep the night before. Eventually he said ok I could go home, but said that I was not to tell my parents what happened, that they would be very hurt, that he and my mother were very good friends. I said all right, provided he didn't do it again to anyone else. But he just shrugged his shoulders and said to me, 'Ah, come on now.' I knew at that moment that I had to do something. I was fifteen then and reasonably secure in myself and definite about my sexuality. If I hadn't been, I think, knowing John, it would have happened again and again. I told my auntie the minute I got back. Luckily, when my dad heard he took it seriously. My mother had to drag him off the shotgun. They were both shattered."

The man who had overseen Fortune's ordination as a priest, Bishop Donal Herlihy, had spent a number of years in Rome, and this, according to those who knew him, gave him a certain sense of style. He loved the classics and liked to spent time translating passages into Greek.

"He was a nice old fella," said one of his priests. "He had been sheltered by being in Rome and wouldn't have had a lot of feeling for the common people."

One visitor to his office remembers that after inviting him to sit down he opened a full bottle of whiskey and proceeded to toss the bottle top into the fireplace. Two glasses sat on the table. The bishop poured some whiskey for himself before pushing the bottle towards his visitor.

Don's father Michael had been in Dr Herlihy's company on many occasions. This time, though, when he made an appointment to see the bishop it was about a very serious matter – the sexual abuse of his son by Fr Sean Fortune. As Don describes it, having been told the story of the meeting by his father, the bishop's reaction was similar to that of Queen Victoria on being advised that there should be a law against lesbianism.

"He didn't believe anything like that could happen, let alone that steps would need to be taken against it."

At the time of that first meeting, Bishop Herlihy was a sick old man.

"What would you suggest that I do with him?" the bishop asked Michael.

"I told him that he needed to send him somewhere that there was a strong parish priest. I suggested that he send him back to Gorey, where he came from, because I felt he would not dirty his own bib. Bishop Herlihy said he could send him on the missions, but he was concerned about the havoc he would create there. Instead he sent him to Poulfur where there was a senior parish priest, and he felt the people were strong there. It never crossed his mind to kick him out. When I had the earlier meeting in St Peter's College, I was going on the basis of things that I had heard were going on there. When I went to Bishop Herlihy it was on the basis of family tragedy."

On a second occasion that Michael spoke to Bishop Herlihy about what Fortune had done to his son, it was at the bishop's own request. "He brought me in again and asked me about it and what could be done. As a result I had this awful feeling that he was making me a part of the decision."

Chapter 4

"Blessed by Father Sean Fortune"

ON THAT DAY in June 1981 when the young curate arrived in Poulfur, his new flock was delighted. Poulfur, located just outside the village of Fethard-on-Sea, was the curacy of the parish of Templetown. Their parish priest, the elderly Canon Willie Mernagh, was widely respected but getting on in years. An energetic, newly ordained curate was just what was needed in this coastal community. As you drive the twenty-five miles from Wexford town to Fethard-on-Sea, approaching the scenic Hook Peninsula on the southernmost tip of the county, the roads become increasingly narrow and winding. The core population here is a few hundred people, but in the summertime visitors swell the population to thousands. Beyond the village, those in the outlying areas live in the most rural part of the county. During the winter months it is undeniably bleak, but when the sun shines on the Hook Peninsula, it is remarkably beautiful.

At the beginning of the 1980s the area was considerably less developed than today and the visitors far fewer in number. However, the new priest seemed excited about the posting, his first in Wexford since his ordination two years previously.

Sean Fortune, as he began to call himself, wasted no time in getting started, arriving to say mass a few days prior to his official starting date. The young Fr Fortune was a tall man standing well over six feet, with a broad smile. He had the confidence now for that full, open smile after having extensive work on his teeth, kindly paid for by a friend after he told her how he was self-conscious about them. His stature caused him to stand out naturally, but in Fethard the sight of him in full soutane, often wearing a skull cap similar to those worn by cardinals, as well as purple socks, made him unmissable. On occasion he could be seen dressed almost totally in white, like the pope. He was rarely without his sunglasses regardless of the time of year, making it impossible to see his blue eyes when you spoke to him.

On Sunday mornings he stood on the altar in St Aidan's Church and gave impassioned sermons, preaching with ease in both English and Irish. Music was an intrinsic part of worship for him, and of the three masses held on a Sunday the first was usually "choir mass", followed by a "folk mass", and then a "song mass". Those who enjoyed the music could bring it home with them by paying £3 for a tape of "The Poulfur Folk Group", recorded singing at the church. Fr Fortune explained that all proceeds from the recording were going to famine relief in Ethiopia.

He began renovations on the parochial house, including the basement, shortly after his arrival. It was in the basement that he invited young boys to gather in the evenings as members of his new Don Bosco Youth Club. Another of the basement rooms in the presbytery was set aside as a refuge for young boys who were having trouble at home.

"It is important for these young lads to have somewhere to go," the priest told parishioners who were caught up in the whirlwind of activity he had created since his arrival.

He could be almost childlike in his efforts to please and quickly became popular with many people, particularly the elderly whom he visited regularly. He impressed others with his kindness in visiting people in hospital, often travelling as far away as Dublin.

One day locals realised he had established, in record time, over thirty local organisations. It was a cause of great pride for him to be at the helm of so many groups in such a small curacy. Reading the parish newsletter, an outsider would have gained the impression that Poulfur was an exceptionally busy city parish. It was crammed full of details of meetings involving the Legion of Mary, the junior Legion of Mary, the Don Bosco Youth Club, Altar Servers, the Ladies' Committee, the Youth Club, Folk Group Training, the No-name Club, the Guide Dog Association, Community Alert, the Pro-life Group, the Ushers' Group, Inter-Marriage Group, Pre-baptism Training Group, Pioneer Total Abstinence Group meetings for adults, with separate meetings for teenagers and nine to twelve year olds. A hierarchy was established in each group, with Fr Fortune at the top, surrounded by the same people. He was generous in the bestowing of titles, such as "top altar boy" and "master of ceremonies".

As well as charting his increasing involvement in the community, the newsletters informed parishioners of trips that had been organised to the Fethard area for groups of young people. Other weeks it was trips away, accompanied by Fr Fortune, for young Fethard teenagers. One week he told parishioners that any family who would like to take a French student, aged twelve to eighteen years old, could do so by applying to himself. He also acted as chaperone for trips to concerts in Dublin. "Boomtown Rats Concert" was the heading in one newsletter. "Bob Geldof of the Boomtown Rats will appear in the RDS on Sunday the 3rd of March in Dublin," it continued. "The cost of the ticket for the concert and the bus all together is £13.00. Applications should be made immediately to the Secretary Parochial House at 97113 and payment for the ticket can be made along with the application."

Fr Fortune was a telecommunications whizz. The number of telephones installed in his house was a matter of local speculation. The figure was put at ten, including one in the toilet. Prior to the introduction of mobile phones, he had a two-way radio in his car, and when they did arrive he was one of the very first to have a mobile. After vigorous fundraising efforts, he bought what was probably one of the first computers in the county, and soon the parish administration was fully computerised.

Traditionally the local newspaper, the *New Ross Standard*, had carried "Fethard Notes", detailing the goings on in the area, but soon Fr Fortune established his own "Poulfur Notes". Each week he wrote promoting his own activities and those of his supporters. Stories featuring him and the latest development he had introduced in the parish began appearing regularly in the local newspapers. He managed to build up a media profile that would be the envy of any politician. One week he announced a plan to stage an annual summer festival on the Hook Peninsula "as big as Slane". He hoped to attract either Chris de Burgh or Bob Geldof, with whom he said he was in school. Another week he called for the introduction of legislation to ban church gate collections by political parties, sporting and other organisations. He described it as "a form of blackmail". People felt a moral obligation to support them, he said. He added that many of those collecting were "hypocrites who are never inside the church itself".

Ecumenical endeavours were one of Fr Fortune's priorities. He held an annual Church Unity Service which always managed to draw high profile people to St Aidan's. One year it was attended by the Bishop of Kildare and Meath, Most Rev. Dr Donal A. Caird. The guest lay speaker on that occasion was "the famous Senator Eoin Ryan of the Ryan family of Tomcoole".

Because of its location, Fethard did not have many activities to keep young people amused, but Fr Fortune did his best to rectify that; however, there were often strings attached if you wanted to participate. A typical arrangement was that a free disco would be held, but nobody could attend who had not obtained a ticket before 7.30pm mass in Poulfur. To be able to qualify for entry to the disco, they had to first attend mass.

Fr Fortune's presence in the area became increasingly difficult to ignore, particularly if you were one of the small but increasing number of people who disliked him. He made his presence felt in so many ways. A well-remembered incident is his putting a lock on the gates of the graveyard. The new arrangement was that visitors would have to call to Fr Fortune's house and ask for the key. A number of families were upset by this and rather than go and ask for the key, they climbed over the wall. After a short time someone, using a bolt cutter, cut the lock off and it was not replaced.

Few could beat Fr Fortune when it came to parting people from their money. It seemed as if the church constantly needed work. A local businessman agreed to donate £2,000 to sponsor a new bell but was afterwards startled to see that the replacement was in fact the old bell which had simply been repaired. One bank holiday weekend, visitors sat among the local congregation and heard an alarming announcement from Fr Fortune, particularly worrying for those sitting in the balcony. He told them that while he did not wish to alarm the people sitting in it, the balcony was unsafe from dry rot and on the point of collapse. A third collection would have to be introduced at mass to pay for its repair. Locals who were familiar with the balcony and knew iron girders held it up were more than a little surprised.

Another Sunday Fr Fortune spoke from the altar about a "heinous crime" which had taken place in the church. He told them the door to the new reconciliation room, where face-to-face confessions were heard, had been stolen over the weekend. He had reported the theft to the police. There were more than a few sniggers when it later emerged that the carpenter who made the door had been the one to "steal" it. He had not been paid for his work and decided, in frustration, to return to the church and reclaim it. Afterwards Fr Fortune made a successful claim on the church insurance.

As well as seeing his name mentioned in the newspapers, parishioners saw it increasingly inscribed on brass plaques, which began appearing in St Aidan's Church, in the grave-yard, at local shrines. Anything that had been blessed, donated or commemorated required a brass plaque with the words "Blessed by Father Sean Fortune" or "In the Curacy of Father Sean Fortune".

When communicating with parishioners, he liked to use flowery language, signing off letters with phrases such as "Your fellow worker in the vineyard of the Lord". A Christmas card sent shortly after his arrival showed a pic-ture of him, as well as one of St Aidan's. Inside was a poem titled "A Priest" which included the lines:

> To have a heart of fire for charity
> And a heart of bronze for chastity,
> To teach and pardon,
> To console and to bless,
> My God what a life!
> And it is yours, Oh Priest of Jesus Christ.

Other poems shared with parishioners included "The Beautiful Hands of a Priest" and "God, Are You Really Real?"

Fr Fortune also liked to travel and once arrived home from a trip with a bottle of water which he said was taken from the River Jordan. His plan was to mingle it with the river that ran alongside St Aidan's so that it would have "all the beneficial effects of the River Jordan and babies could be baptised there".

In those days masses were said in the area "at the drop of a hat" and blessings bestowed at some of the most unusual occasions, causing concern among some people that he was actually abusing the sacraments. Others dis-agreed, feeling it demonstrated his enthusiasm for his ministry. This enthusiasm spilled over into the introduction of some previously unheard of feast days and confusion of the saints, such as "mass in honour of the sacred heart of St Bridget".

Requests for money appeared regularly in the newsletters. A "parish chancellor" was appointed, and his job was to cycle around the parish and collect dues from those who were slow to pay. Parishioners were admonished by the chancellor for not returning the envelopes and told that Fr Fortune had instructed they would be "levied" in future. In mass additional collections were held, and the concept of a "silent collection" was introduced to Poulfur church for the first time. Fr Fortune seemed to need an awful lot of money; however, even doubters might have been reassured when they opened their local newspaper and saw how much he was achieving with it.

At that time the Irish economy was in a depressed state. Unemployment was high, particularly in an area like Fethard. The priest told his congregation that something had to be done. Being the man of action that he was, he went to ANCO, then the training authority which would become FÁS when it amalgamated with the National Manpower Service and the Youth Employment Agency. He persuaded them of the need to introduce community employment schemes to the area. He said he would act as administrator.

The curate never appeared to have a shortage of money himself. He had an apartment in Dublin and liked big cars, driving them somewhat recklessly on the winding country roads. He had a number of accidents, but it was never long before he would have a bigger and better replacement. After one car accident he ended up on crutches and told parishioners that because of the injury he could not genuflect. At mass an altar boy would put a stool in front of him so that he could rest his leg on it. One Sunday a number of mass-goers, who had heard he was suing for compensation for his injuries, could hardly stifle their giggles when he got up and walked without difficulty around the altar before suddenly remembering the crutch.

Not long after his arrival in the summer of 1981, a row broke out that would cause a number of people to realise that as well as being bright, energetic and often charming, he was also manipulative and a bully. It seems almost ludicrous from this remove that such strife could result from a row concerning control of a small parish hall, but even today the repercussions of what happened can be felt. This was to set a marker for the rest of Fr Sean Fortune's time in Fethard. People ended up on two well-defined sides: those who were with the priest and those who were against him. Nobody, it appears, held a position anywhere in between.

At that time Sean Cloney was the chairman of the committee which ran the village hall. "Out of courtesy, I gave him a key to the hall and we offered him a place on the committee," he explained. "At a meeting we said he would be welcome to use the hall on certain nights when there were no other activities and things were flexible. Fr Fortune got up and thanked us but said he could use the hall any night he wanted because it was 'parochial property'. He said he had the deeds and would bring them to the next meeting, showing that the bishop owned it and he could run it. It was clear from the start that he wanted control."

The next meeting, said Sean, was even more turbulent. "He brought the deeds and waved them around. He was asked to read out the relevant paragraph. He never liked to be challenged. He would not accept what we said."

Between meetings he had tried to put pressure on Sean Cloney. Refusing to knuckle under, the chairman read out a statement which explained the developments and said that "an evil influence" had come into the parish. He then adjourned the meeting so people could consider their position. "But Fortune stood up and insisted that he wanted to speak, saying anyone that left was 'defying the priest'."

Half the members stayed, and after that the committee was divided. An AGM was called and notices were put in the local paper about an election of trustees because of the "confusion in the parish". In the midst of it all, Fr Fortune had the locks on the hall door changed. He also wrote to the insurers saying he was taking over the policy and paid the next year's premium.

"It all sounds so farcical now when I look back," says another committee member, "but it was typical of the way he operated. He told us we would not be allowed into the hall until we acknowledged him as head of it. The situation was complicated by the fact that Macra na Feirme had booked a disco the following weekend and Fortune said he was holding his own disco there. At the same time he had arranged a function in the local hotel."

Macra had advertised their disco with posters hung from poles in the village. Mysteriously, in the days running up to the event, they began disappearing.

Macra members devised a strategy for that night. It involved lying in wait for the DJ. When he arrived and began bringing his equipment into the hall, they took their chance to slip inside. Once this was accomplished they set up their table at the door and began to collect money. Sean Cloney explained what happened next.

"Fortune, decked out in the full clerical gear, came rushing up. Beside him was a young clerical student who was a regular visitor to his home. He was told he would have to pay if he wanted to go inside. He turned away in fury saying, 'A Catholic priest locked out of his own hall.' Back at the hotel he was raging and told the people there that the firstborn of the Macra people would be deformed."

Deputy Hugh Byrne, Fianna Fáil TD in the area for many years, remembers that his first meeting with the priest coincided exactly with this latest twist in the hall saga. Fr Fortune had telephoned earlier in the week and asked him to judge a competition he had organised in the local hotel for that night. Close to the appointed time, Byrne was on his way there. He was walking up the street when, suddenly, he saw a tall man coming quickly towards him. As he got closer he recognised that it was a priest. In fact, it was Fortune who was just returning from the confrontation with Macra at the hall. Stopping abruptly in front of him, Fortune asked the TD if he was the chairman of the local Macra branch. When Hugh Byrne answered that he was, the response was swift and short: "Well, you can fuck off home with yourself."

Attempting a different strategy, the hall committee had the locks changed. A deputation went to the then bishop, Dr Herlihy. During the meeting, the group offered to deposit the key with him until after the election of new members.

"He told us we were the lawful committee and that he had never sent 'that man' into the parish to interfere. He banged the table then and said, 'God help him.' But nothing happened after, and Fortune then insisted Bishop Herlihy had appointed him administrator of the hall. He told people in the community to book the hall through him," said Sean Cloney.

"The truth meant nothing to him. We put up a notice in the hall window detailing what the bishop had said. Of course there was awful trouble: 90 per cent of people would never think that the priest would lie, and who could blame them? That was the way things were. From the start he bitterly divided the parish."

One evening shortly after Fortune's arrival, a man who was involved in the Boy Scouts approached Sean Cloney in the street. "He said that word had come through about things that had happened in St Peter's College, and that under no circumstances was Fortune to be allowed into the Scouts. The conclusion I drew was that there was something improper. After that I kept my eyes and ears open and observed things."

Another man involved in the hall committee at that time, who had also been part of the deputation to Dr Herlihy, said that the committee had come under tremendous pressure as they were seen by many to be going against the priest. Matters were not improved with the election of a new committee.

The row was reported in the local newspaper, and subsequently letters were published. One letter, in favour of the priest, signed by "An Outside Observer", said that since Fortune's arrival in the parish it was his aim to involve the entire community in the everyday running of the area under his care, and that in doing so he may have "tread on a few toes—toes that just happen to belong to a few who felt the parish couldn't function without their involvement".

It continued: "Those concerned were and are some of the more influential (in financial terms) people in the area, who in true Christian fashion objected to sharing a place at the table (hall committee) with their neighbours, who they judged not by their ability to do the job well and with genuine commitment, but by the size of the car or the number of acres owned by the individual concerned."

On the same letters page, Sean Cloney wrote to clarify some of the facts contained in a previous report about the hall AGM. He pointed out that the current members of the committee had not resigned but rather had not stood for re-election.

Later in the letter Sean referred to an assertion made by the priest that young people of the area should not be out after a certain hour. Fr Fortune had written in a parish newsletter that if parents really cared about their teenage sons and daughters, they should keep them off the streets after 9pm on weekend nights. "It is simply dangerous from many points of view. If you don't care that's your responsibility," he told them.

"It was rather strange then," said Sean Cloney's letter, "for him to advertise a disco and barbecue in the sand-hills of the Big Burrow last Sunday night, where many young-sters were frolicking at 2 a.m. on Monday morning. Since Fr Fortune was a mile and a half away in Fethard village at 1.30 a.m. it would seem that the much vaunted 'clerical supervision' was a false promise. Parents have reason for serious concern but let nobody blame the hall or its pres-ent management committee."

This letter was followed up by a letter from other mem-bers of the committee further explaining what had gone on. In it they thanked "An Outside Observer" for giving them an opportunity to give a true account of some of the diffi-culties they had to overcome. "We are prepared to stand over this letter by our signatures, unlike 'An Outside Observer' and whosoever inspired him or her to put pen to paper."

Hugh Byrne explains that in his position as a rural TD he was almost automatically appointed "chairman of every-thing" until Fortune arrived in the area and quickly began to insist that he was the one who should hold that posi-tion. "It didn't bother me. I had more than enough to be doing, but the trouble and divisions started straightaway. At one stage I had the hall committee and Fortune up to my house to try and sort it out, but I think now it actually made matters worse. He was adamant."

The rows continued and with them the strife between members of the community. There were some who would not hear a bad word against Fr Fortune, but also those who thought the day would never come when he would be moved away. However, these people learned to be care-ful, because those that he believed were against him could find themselves being denounced from the altar.

His arrival in June 1981 had been after the traditional time for the Corpus Christi procession, but the priest insisted that he wanted one held anyway. He also changed the venue from Poulfur to a bigger procession in Fethard vil-lage. He insisted that he wanted Macra na Feirme members to steward the parade. It was pointed out to him that his approach was somewhat insensitive since some members of Macra were Protestant and that the location where he wanted to put the procession stage had Church of Ireland people living right alongside. However, he was insistent, saying that members of Macra were happy enough to use the community hall, which was church property.

His bore his grudge against Macra publicly. The organisation continued to be a thorn in his side since it was one of the very few that remained outside of his control. One Sunday he even refused to give communion to a young Macra member during mass in Poulfur. At that time Ferns was without a bishop, as Bishop Comiskey had not yet replaced Bishop Herlihy, who had died in April 1983. The vicar general, Monsignor William Shiggins, now deceased, was in charge. A man who had been on the hall deputation to Bishop Herlihy spoke to Monsignor Shiggins about the young Macra member and the communion incident.

"His mother, who was a very pious woman, went to see Fortune one night, and she remonstrated with him about what he had done. She got no satisfaction. He more or less pushed her out the door into the yard, and since it was so dark she stumbled on the grave of a former curate. Her husband, who had been waiting in the car, then went to speak to Fortune – but again no luck. This episode came to the attention of the hall committee. I knew Monsignor Shiggins personally, so I went to see him. He asked me what I wanted him to do. I told him he should come out and talk to the family. But all he did when he met them was to say that he was very sorry and that it should not have happened and that they were good people. He advised them to go to Templetown to mass instead of Poulfur. I don't know if he reprimanded yer man. It would have been useless."

One of the other organisations that was successful in keeping him out was the local GAA club, St Mogue's. Fr

Fortune turned up in the dressing room one Sunday before a hurling match in New Ross, saying he wanted to bless the team before the game. After this, on the way out, he bent to pick up the spare hurleys and was heading for the sideline when he was stopped by a man involved in training the team.

"I told him that I was in charge of the hurleys. He thought damn hard about it, but he had clashed with me before and he knew that I meant it. After that he kept away from us," explained the man.

A year after his arrival Fr Fortune was a witness in the district court in a case concerning a licence for an amusement arcade in the parish. Objecting to the licence, he told the judge that "gaming machines could lead to a temptation to abandon love and justice as portrayed in the Gospel" and that their presence in Fethard-on-Sea would be detrimental to the area. He went on to paint a picture of Fethard that was extreme by any standards.

"I spent my first summer taking drug addicts off the street. I took young people who were drunk off the street and tried to rehabilitate them. I was curate in Courtown for a number of years [This is untrue; Fortune never served as curate in Courtown.] and lived with the problem of young people stealing money from their own homes to play these gaming machines. It is my opinion that the quality of life in the village would suffer greatly from one of these halls."

As a discussion was being held between counsel and the presiding judge about a second court date, Fortune, speaking from his seat, announced that a particular day being considered was not convenient for him. "I'm afraid that doesn't suit me," he said. "I'm in Liverpool concelebrating mass with the pope."

Despite his impassioned protests about the arcade, the licence was granted. A few months later those assembled for its official opening in Fethard were bemused to see the curate, so publicly opposed to the venture, giving it his blessing.

Since his arrival in the area, Fortune's relationship with the parish priest, Canon Willie Mernagh, had not been great. Canon Mernagh was a priest in the traditional sense and his only outside interest was the GAA. At one time he was chairman of the Wexford county board. The relationship between the pair was to become so fraught that his efforts to control Fr Fortune were also written about in the local newspapers. In 1983 a report was carried that Canon Mernagh had objected in court to an application by Fortune for a lottery licence for a 300 Club Draw. The incredulous judge described it as "trade jealousy in the Church".

"You would imagine that the parish priest and the curate would have settled this without coming into court. It is more like fiction than fact. The curate wants a licence and the parish priest is objecting because he already has a licence for the same funds. It will make history," said the judge before granting the application to Fortune.

Chapter 5

A Parish Divided

"FROM THE START we knew there was something wrong," said a Fethard-on-Sea man recalling the arrival of Fr Sean Fortune to the area. "He came into the parish and he just wanted to take over. He had ways of finding out about people, recognising weakness and family things that people preferred to keep private. His policy was to divide and conquer, and he was the most incredible bully. He would burst his way into anything. If he could not control an organisation, he would set one up in opposition. There was an evilness there which is still frightening to think of. We tried for years to get something done about him, but it felt as if nobody was listening. Now we know that there was even worse going on all the time with the sex abuse. It is still difficult to comprehend."

Why did the late Bishop of Ferns, Dr Donal Herlihy, decide to visit a person as obviously troublesome as Fr Sean Fortune on the people of Fethard-on-Sea? His predecessor in Poulfur, Fr Joshua Kilty, may have had the answer.

"Josh was a lovely man," said Sean Cloney. "He was a painter and a great character, and God knows we have had them in Poulfur."

Fr Kilty, now deceased, told Sean that the bishop's logic in sending Fr Fortune there was because "he had the sea on three sides of him and a crusty parish priest on the other side. It was seen as the best way of isolating him." When he arrived, Fr Fortune said he was only there for three months, but as it happened he remained for six years.

As was subsequently discovered, Bishop Herlihy's plan, if it could be described as such, failed abysmally. There were numerous complaints over the years covering everything from the priest's putting curses on people to sexual abuse. However, once it had been put in place, it seemed that making any change was virtually impossible. Bishop Herlihy and his successor, Bishop Brendan Comiskey, who arrived in the diocese in April 1984, appeared to those involved at that time to be unable to activate an alternative plan. In the background efforts were being made, but those on the ground did not see the evidence of them.

Sit a Fethard person down, ask them about Fr Fortune, and you could find yourself sitting there three hours later, the stories still not dried up. They are sad stories of abuse, not just sexual abuse, but also stories of bullying and intimidation and of vulnerable people being conned out of money and possessions. However, you could also find yourself laughing out loud at some of his other antics. Even with those he sexually abused, there are invariably moments of laughter when that person, recounting yet another ridiculous episode, realises the absolute daftness of it all and begins to giggle. In Fethard-on-Sea they need their sense of humour.

For a small seaside village the place has seen its fair share of excitement over the decades, almost all of it involving Catholic priests. When Sean Cloney said he had his "own trouble with the clergy in the 1950s", it was an understatement. He was the man whose early married life was recently captured on celluloid in the movie *A Love Divided*. The movie told the story of a boycott of Protestant businesses in Fethard in the 1950s which came about as a result of the interference of a priest in the marriage of Sean and his wife Sheila.

A Parish Divided

Sean, a Catholic, and Sheila Kelly, a member of the Church of Ireland, were neighbours. They attended the local Catholic school together, and their farming families were friendly. In their teenage years they began to go out together. It was the beginning of their difficulties. The local curate put pressure on Sean to break off the relationship. He demurred. Recognising the difficulty of marrying locally, Sean and Sheila married in a registry office in England. Later they married in a Catholic church and Sheila signed a document stating that any children born would be raised Catholic.

The couple returned to Fethard and had two daughters, Eileen and Mary. In January 1957, when Eileen was coming up to the time when she would go to school, Sheila received a visit from the local priest, Fr William Stafford. He told her that her children would be going to the Catholic school and there was nothing she could do about it.

"Sheila didn't fancy being ordered," explained Sean. "She developed the frame of mind, 'We'll see what can be done about it.'"

As the pressure mounted, Sean knew that his wife was thinking of leaving. "It was not up to me to restrain her," he said simply. One day at the end of April, he came in from the farm at lunchtime to find her and the children gone. With £70 in her pocket, half of it earned by selling some of the pigs two days earlier, she fled. A few days later Sean received a visit from an associate of Ian Paisley. He presented Sean with an ultimatum: if he wanted to save his marriage he would have to emigrate to either Canada or Australia, agree to his children being brought up as Protestants and consider changing his own religion.

Sean refused and began legal proceedings for the return of the children. The story then took a different turn when Sheila and the children were moved to the Orkney Islands in Scotland. In Fethard-on-Sea feelings were running high.

A boycott of local Protestant businesses began. Towards the end of May an anonymous letter appeared in *The Irish Times.*

"I wonder is your paper aware of the trouble and worry which is being suffered by the Protestant people of Fethard as a result of this case. They are being ostracised, their shops (two of them) are completely boycotted, their children without a school. The teacher of the Protestant school is a Roman Catholic and was threatened with stoning if she continued to teach."

An article on the boycott was carried in *Time* magazine that August. It quoted Galway's Bishop Michael Browne, responding to some lay Catholics who suggested that the hierarchy come out against what was being described as "fethardism": "Non-Catholics do not protest against the crime of conspiring to steal the children of a Catholic father, but they try to make political capital when a Catholic people make a peaceful and moderate protest." The boycott received worldwide attention and was raised in the Dáil, in the British House of Commons and in Stormont. Taoiseach Eamonn de Valera said the whole thing was "ill-conceived, ill-considered and futile".

One of the first victims was Sheila's father, a cattle dealer who found people would not sell cattle to him. His sin? He had given his daughter £40 before she left. Sean felt particularly strongly about the attack on Mr Kelly who was, he said, an outstandingly generous man.

"What they overlooked was that this same man gave a blank cheque to a local Catholic boy who lost an arm so that he could buy a business. He was ruined and he later died of a broken heart."

Sean tried to fight the boycott with the assistance of a few old IRA men who had fallen out with the clergy during the War of Independence, but to no avail. A few months later, Sheila's father and the local TD, a Knight of Columbanus, issued a joint statement, the local priest went into the shop most affected to buy a packet of cigarettes and the boycott was over.

It took longer for Sean to extricate his wife from the grip of the Paisleyites. Eventually the couple were reconciled and after some time in England returned home. However, the matter of the education of their children remained.

"Whether they went to a Protestant or a Catholic school would have been seen as a victory for one side or the other, so they never went to school and we educated them ourselves," said Sean.

Reconciliation came more slowly to Fethard-on-Sea, and finally, it came through the two families who had been such close friends and neighbours. Sheila's brother had a little girl who was born with a hole in her heart. She had to go to London for an operation, where she died, aged three. Her body was brought home for burial. Two of Sheila's sisters had also married Catholics, and so three of the child's pall bearers were her Catholic uncles. They walked up the avenue towards the Protestant church, where Protestant men were waiting to take the coffin, because at the time Catholics were not allowed to enter a Protestant church.

"That little coffin had a three-year-old child in it, our niece. I went into the church with the coffin and the other two men followed suit. When they saw that, other Catholics came in. It was a milestone," said Sean. During the years Sheila continued to go to services at the Church of Ireland and Sean to mass.

A Love Divided brought the reality of the boycott home to people, some too young to remember that it had ever happened. However, it also reopened old wounds for many in the area who bitterly resented its all being raked up again. The publicising of the exploits of Fr Sean Fortune brings a similar reaction. The bitter history of the parish makes the original decision to post Sean Fortune there all the more baffling.

In later years, Sean Fortune would try to blame the problems in Fethard on the boycott, claiming that criticism of him was of his doctrinal stance, "derived from the rather tense atmosphere that still remained in the town from these earlier troubles", according to Dr Christie Brown.

In the way of small parishes in rural Ireland, Hugh Byrne, as a TD, frequently found himself in the company of the priest, and his impression of him from their first meeting did not improve.

"Almost everyone has redeeming qualities, but it is hard to identify one in him. He did have a lot of energy, but really he was an overbearing bully. It may seem like I am only saying this in hindsight, but none of the young people liked him. There was never a shortage of money wherever he got it from. He always drove a big car. He could crash it today and have a new one tomorrow, and he would crash that in a few months' time. He had no conscience about taking money from people, including tricking them out of it."

At that time, as well as preying on young boys such as Don from outside the area, Fortune was turning his attention to local boys. Sean Cloney remembers one family who lived close by and had always attended mass in Poulfur church. Around 1982, for no known reason, they could be seen driving past the church to go to Templetown for mass.

"I knew something was wrong. Then I heard Fortune had been messing with the boy who had joined his youth club, and everything fell into place. I mentioned it to a few people I could trust. I knew if I tried to do anything I could be sued. I had no evidence, nobody to stand behind me. I know that it may seem strange nowadays, but he had the parish divided. There were those who supported him and thought he was perfect. The rest of us who did not think that way used to hint that there was something 'funny' about him. I would say there were quite a lot of people uncomfortable, but they did not dare open their mouths."

The boy whose family had changed from mass in Poulfur to Templetown was Jim (not his real name). At that
time he was a shy seventeen year old and he remembers
clearly what he suffered at the hands of Fr Fortune. The
episode occurred on a winter night in January 1982. The
priest asked Jim to accompany him home because he was
afraid he would get stuck in the snow. He promised he
would drive him home in the morning.

When they arrived at the house, the priest took Jim to a
bedroom where there was one large bed and a single bed.
Since it was a very cold night they should both sleep
together in the large bed, said Fr Fortune. Since Jim had
often shared a bed with his brothers, he didn't think the
notion strange. He drifted off to sleep but then woke to
find Fr Fortune's hands on his penis. Pretending to be
asleep he pushed the arm away. Waking again sometime
later, he found his hand had been manoeuvered behind his
back in such a way that it was touching the priest's erect
penis, while his own penis was also being fondled. Jim
immediately tried to jump from the bed, saying he just
wanted to go home, but Fr Fortune held him down and
began apologising for his behaviour. Eventually he disen-
tangled himself and began to dress. Fr Fortune jumped up
and barred his way, locking the door. He told Jim that it
was too cold to go home and that if he would just get into
the other bed and go to sleep nothing else would happen.
Jim acquiesced but found it impossible to sleep.

In the morning when he got up, Fr Fortune offered him
breakfast. While sitting at the table, the priest took out a
Bible and insisted that Jim swear he would not tell anyone
what had occurred the previous night. If that meant he
could get out of there sooner, he would do it, so he swore
on the Bible. He was terrified.

Once he got home he went straight to his room. His
sister Angela (not her real name), who had followed him
up, saw that he was distressed and asked him what had

happened. He confided the horrible episode to her. Downstairs Fr Fortune, who had followed him inside, was talking to his parents. After he left, Angela told her shocked mother what had gone on. Jim remembers that his mother was very supportive and told him that he was not the first person something like that had happened to. After that the subject never came up in conversation. Not only was Jim too embarrassed and shocked to go to the gardaí, but at the time he did not know what had happened was a crime. He remembers Fr Fortune as being manipulative and powerful and someone you would be afraid to contradict. He had respect for authority, particularly for priests. It was what his parents had taught him.

When Paul Molloy was in sixth class, he used to have a recurring nightmare. He was on the school bus on his way home from school and looking ahead he would see Fr Fortune standing on the side of the road. The priest would put his hand out and stop the bus. Boarding it, he would say to the bus driver that he was taking Paul into his car. In his sleep the youngster would feel the horrible sense of dread. He knew what would happen once the priest got him on his own.

For Paul the nightmare was a horrible reality that began when he was around eleven years old. His mother was delighted when he told her he wanted to be an altar boy. It meant that he was now in Fr Fortune's company a lot, but usually with a group that the priest would invite to his house, just beside the church. One evening Paul was the only one to be invited. Fr Fortune began to talk to him about puberty and how young boys change. He had a chart that would tell if Paul was developing properly, but to do so Fr Fortune would need to check him. On that occasion the priest just looked. Afterwards he gave Paul a hug and said they were the best of friends.

He persuaded Paul to join the Legion of Mary and the Don Bosco Youth Club, which met in the basement of his house around three times a week. Paul began to receive regular invitations to stay back, and the abuse got progressively worse. It never seemed strange to anyone that Fr Fortune constantly sought out his company because, as Paul explains, he was a priest.

"Fr Fortune started open confession in the church and then assaulted me during confession. It didn't matter where he was, he was always on the lookout for opportunities. I would read at first mass and he would abuse me before second mass, blessing the Eucharist an hour later. He would leave messages all the time with my mother, saying that he wanted to see me. My main concern was that nobody should know what was happening. I was ashamed. I was in constant fear, never knowing where he would be. There were two different Fr Fortunes: the priest who would go up to the altar and give terrific sermons about the evils of drink, sex and sin, and the other one who would talk to young boys about homosexuality and sex, interview them one by one—asking them questions that never should have been asked—and abuse them. It didn't matter where he was or what he was, he was always on the lookout for opportunities. My main concern was never to let anybody know and he knew that. But I knew what would happen as soon as I went down there. He would use every and any excuse that you can think of and, of course, as a priest that never seemed strange."

When he moved to secondary school, Paul tried to get out of being an altar boy, but Fr Fortune would not let him because he could not give a good reason why. Instead he made him a reader at mass. One day he invited Paul to go away for a weekend. Paul felt safe because the priest said his brother would also be travelling. Arrangements were made with Paul's mother, who dropped him down to the house that Friday evening. It was then Fr Fortune told Paul that his brother was not able to make the trip and that it would just be the two of them. They would leave the next day.

That night the abuse began while they were watching television and got progressively worse when they moved to the bedroom. It was the first and last time that Paul was in that room. Afterwards, while the priest slept, he recalls being in a state of shock. He stayed awake all night, making up his mind that he was not going to Bray with Fr Fortune the next morning.

As soon as the priest woke, Paul said that he was feeling unwell and had a pain in his stomach. After breakfast he went to the bathroom and made himself vomit using his fingers. Fr Fortune asked him to reconsider his decision not to come on the trip but the young boy was adamant. He said he would bring Paul home but dropped him a few hundred yards from the house. Paul told his mother he was sick.

Although the abuse continued, after youth club meetings and mass on Sunday, Paul made every effort to avoid Fortune and it became less frequent. It helped that he was now at secondary school. Around this time Fr Fortune began to give him money, usually around £10, which Paul sometimes refused. The priest offered to increase the amounts significantly if Paul allowed him to continue to sexually abuse him. At one point he offered to leave the priesthood if Paul would marry him.

In September 1984 Paul turned fourteen. He decided that the abuse had to stop. He told Fr Fortune that if it did not he would tell the gardaí. The priest retaliated by saying that it would be Paul's word against his and that it had been consenting sex.

"How could I consent?" asks Paul. "I was only a boy."

The priest steered clear of him for a few months, but one day he asked Paul if the two of them "were still the best of friends" and tried to give him a hug. It was the end of the abuse, although as a mass reader and member of the youth club, Paul remained in contact with Fortune.

"I was living in constant fear of him and I was afraid to tell my parents what was happening to me because he was a priest and I was afraid nobody would believe me because of him being a priest. Looking back on it now his behaviour was so inappropriate and so unbelievably outrageous."

Those in Fethard who had their suspicions but no proof about the sexual abuse of young boys were afraid to speak out. They were too well aware of Fr Fortune's ability to manipulate a situation and wriggle his way out of it. He used any and every method to throw people off balance, including the taping of conversations. A garda who once went to speak to him in the parish house in Poulfur about a routine matter told of how, when he returned to base, his superintendent told him that the priest had called to make a complaint about the garda. Fr Fortune was able to quote exactly what had been said during the conversation. The garda was advised that the next time he went to visit the priest to "play it by the book" and bring someone else with him. On another occasion, when the priest left the room the garda walked around to the other side of the desk and saw a tape recorder was indeed running in the desk drawer.

"I'd say a lot of them couldn't believe what he was up to and got away with," says a man who lived outside of Fethard but was familiar with the area. "It was the things to do with money that bothered most of them. You have to remember that it was not that long since the boycott. I think that is why people kept records of his time there. The place was still divided. This just caused further division."

The garda was not the only one that Fortune used the tape recorder as a weapon against. One evening a fourteen-year-old local boy was in the priest's sitting room when Fr Fortune began to feel his penis and urged him to do the same to him. He offered him alcohol from the drinks cabinet and began to ask him questions. Would the boy go to bed with his friend? Going further, he asked if he would do so under the influence of alcohol? The boy replied that he had never been drunk and did not know how much control he would lose. Later that evening Fortune told him that he had taped their conversation, as well as conversations held previously. At one point the priest offered that boy £150 to do gardening and maintenance work around the house and told him that if he did well in his Intermediate Certificate he would buy him a motorbike, and a car if he performed well in his Leaving Certificate. He always asked the boy how he was getting on with his girlfriend and exactly what he did with her when they were alone together. He would keep looking to see if the boy became aroused during the conversations.

Another boy remembers Fortune telling him that he wanted to have a chat with him about sex education. He was going to talk to everyone in the youth club because he was concerned about any local girls getting pregnant, he said. He kept asking questions about what the boy had done sexually with his girlfriend. Occasionally, said the boy, he had fondled her breasts and on one occasion had dared to put his hand between her legs, for which he received a slap across the face. After hearing the story Fortune told the boy he would never be able to look the girl's father in the face again without telling him about what had occurred. The boy was shocked and scared. Fortune asked him if he had ever slept with his girlfriend, or with anyone else. The boy replied that he had not. If a friend asked him to sleep with them, said the priest, what would he say? The boy said that if she were nice enough he probably would accept. The conversation then turned to whether he had ever slept with a boy. He said he had shared a bed with his cousin when he came on holidays. Fortune asked him if he got erections during those times. The boy said it had never happened. Just then Fortune asked him if he trusted him and if he would sleep with him. The frightened boy said he wanted to leave straightaway. Fortune said he could leave, but first he (Fortune) would swear on the Bible not to repeat anything he had heard to the girl's parents. Then he directed the boy to put his right hand on the Bible and swear that he would repeat nothing that had been said during the conversation.

As with practically all paedophiles, Fortune managed through threats and bribery to keep the abuse a secret. However, his other activities were getting to such a level that an organised opposition began to emerge. Kieran (not his real name), a Fethard man, had become a member of the parish hall committee after the original committee stood down. He and some others on the committee became fed up of what he described as the "strange carryings-on of Fr Fortune". Kieran says that when he and other members of the new committee had gone to speak to Bishop Herlihy, following in the steps of the previous committee, he had essentially agreed with what they had to say. "We went home and then we noticed the way that Fortune was continuing to carry on, so I wrote to the bishop some time later, stating that the committee would welcome a further meeting. We used diplomatic language in that letter because we did not want to be seen to be anti-clerical," explains Kieran.

But still, apparently, no action was taken and the situation worsened. In July 1983 Kieran and other members of the committee decided to write to the then papal nuncio, Dr Gaetano Alibrandi. This effort followed the death of Bishop Herlihy and was prior to the appointment of Dr Brendan Comiskey as Bishop of Ferns. Armed with a considerable knowledge of canon law, Kieran drew up a letter signed by himself and three of the hall committee members, requesting that a Church enquiry be held into the administration of the Poulfur curacy, and explaining why it was necessary.

Your Excellency,

It is with deep anxiety that, in the absence of a diocesan Bishop (Dr D. Herlihy decd.), we beg you to promote a diligent enquiry, at the earliest opportunity, into the administration of the Poulfur curacy, Templetown parish, Diocese of Ferns, Co Wexford.

Since the posting here, in June 1981, of Fr Sean Fortune cc, there has been a succession of "incidents" of public conflict between curate and laity, all involving the purported supremacy of ecclesiastical authority over the people of Fethard-On-Sea and the area generally in matters non-ecclesiastical. As the Church, in our view of Vatican II, consists of all the people of God, we are perturbed by the continuing authoritarianism of Fr Fortune, the curate. He has aroused very much conflict among Catholic people of the area, right across the social and economic spectrum.

At this stage it would be premature to present in detail, a list of allegations which we would formulate to any persons charged with due authority to conduct the enquiry which we are requesting. We have been reluctant, until now, to bring such "charges" into the open in deference to an ordained priest and in the hope of a possible attenuation of Father Fortune's attitude, and for fear of supernatural repercussions. However recent pulpit pronouncements, church newsletter statements and open campaign against the Community (the People's Hall), has forced us to take this action. This anti-Hall campaign, is being conducted and orchestrated by Fr Fortune, who has publicly "cursed" the Hall Management Committee, even from the Altar.

The blatantly obvious object of his anger currently, is the Community Hall Management Committee, however, this is but his thinly veiled wrath at many local people, who continue to resist what they consider his insincerity of motive, and his disclared [*sic*] policy of manipulation, his methods leads us to the conclusion that "money" and his unquestionable use of it, appears to be his primary consideration.

Fr Fortune is very young and active, and possibly could be a holy man, but he is wholly out of place in a rural parish structure which entrusts the curacy with responsibility of a large and mature community – without adequate effective supervision or checks on his authoritarian behaviour, without prejudice or disrespect to our Parish Priest – Rev. Wm. Mernagh P.P. We feel very strongly, as do many local people, that the curate is unsuited to our rural parish, and we respectfully beg Your Excellency to bring the matter before the competent Ecclesiastical Authorities with due urgency, so that a committee of Enquiry, or its equivalent, could be instituted, at your earliest convenience – at which time we shall be willing to produce substantiating evidence.

Sincerely yours,

Under the four signatures it was indicated that copies of the letter had been sent to Cardinal Tomás Ó Fiaich, Monsignor William Shiggins, who was based in New Ross, and Canon Mernagh.

Billy Moroney from New Ross, who had known Fortune as a clerical student during summers spent in Duncannon, came across him again during the campaign for the 1983 abortion referendum. Billy was a member of the anti-amendment pro-choice campaign. He remembers being approached by people from Fethard who felt that the priest had gone, somewhat typically, overboard. An article written in August 1983 by a reporter from *The Irish Times,* Judy Doherty, gave an insight into what was going on in the area. Doherty wrote that on the altar with Fr Sean Fortune in Fethard-on-Sea that Sunday morning was a woven cradle and in it a life-sized baby doll tucked beneath a blanket, its plastic arms outstretched. A sign attached to the cradle bore the words: "Thou shalt not kill." The sermon that morning was given by a young seminarian under Fr Fortune's tutelage.

The Church, he said, "is the supreme moral authority over every other institution . . . It is a divine right given to her." Calling the referendum a moral issue, the seminarian continued: "The Church is much more competent to speak than the State . . . the priest has the obligation to preach . . . Thou shalt not kill." He went on to say that the amendment would separate the sheep from the goats, and warned that the Church might appear archaic in its support of the amendment. "The people will have to make a decision on whether they are for the Church or against it," adding that they were "putting God on trial". After mass altar boys stood at the church exits and handed out pro-amendment leaflets.

Outside at the entrance to the church grounds, members of the anti-amendment campaign stood urging people to reject it because it could threaten the lives of pregnant women if doctors were forced to choose between the woman and the foetus. Among them was Eileen Kehoe, formerly Cloney. At her own church that morning, her mother Sheila Cloney was also leafleting. Eileen explained that they had chosen to fight the amendment although they had realised that their involvement could be a reminder, both to those who could barely remember and those who would like to forget, of the events that had occurred previously in Fethard.

"The divisions in the community were very obvious from the start when we went to Fethard to campaign," says Billy Moroney. "It was riven apart by Fortune. In Fethard the issue of abortion was nothing compared to where you stood on the priest. While I was down there, I started to hear disturbing stories about young boys. People came to me, but at that time they didn't say right out what they thought was happening. Youngsters who were very outgoing and happy had become very withdrawn. They were giving their parents trouble. It disturbed me. The common thread through the stories was Sean Fortune. He always wanted to surround himself with boys. He would never have two of them on the altar if he could have ten. Everything about the situation seemed strange. I mentioned it to a few people, including a garda in New Ross. He was shocked – shocked at me for saying such a thing and disgusted that I had even suggested it," says Billy, who was a member of the Labour Party and had stood as a general election candidate in February 1982 and in a few Seanad elections.

Judging from the abortion referendum results, Fortune's efforts backfired somewhat. Although almost three-quarters of people in Wexford voted "Yes", in rural Fethard-on-Sea almost half of the electorate voted "No". It was a disappointment, especially compared to Blackwater, County Wexford, where the local priest had prayed and fasted in support of the amendment. The "Yes" vote there was 86 per cent.

Not long after the referendum, Moroney came across the priest again. His son, who was attending secondary school in New Ross, told him that the priest was giving a retreat to his class. "I told my son and I told him to tell his friends not to end up in a situation where they were alone with him. Of course, teenagers being what they are, they made every effort to do so. Afterwards my son would never tell us for years what had gone on. Of course Fortune had compromised them. He handed out a questionnaire, and one of the questions asked them if they were one of the 95 per cent of boys who masturbated or the 5 per cent who lied and said they didn't. At one point he put a £5 on the table and said it would go to the boy who could shock him with the most outrageous stories. Of course the boys went to town with the stories. Then he asked them questions about where they had 'put' their penises. Some of those lads didn't even know what masturbating was. Of course he was able to recognise the vulnerable ones and he zoned in on them. I think he had the rest of the lads twigged, but he picked on two or three boys. One of the teachers told me afterwards that if they had known at the time what had gone on, not only would they have thrown him out but they would have had him arrested."

A Message from Heaven

In Fethard, Kieran and his friends, who were still awaiting a response to their letter to the papal nuncio, heard that the nuncio was to visit nearby Kilmore Quay. After explaining the situation to the local priest there, they travelled to meet the nuncio and present their case in person. Kieran explains what happened: "We told him that we were not competent to inquire into these matters under canon law. We felt that it should be done properly and a tribunal of inquiry held. Alibrandi told us he would look into it. He assured us that Rome was fully aware of the situation and was concerned at our plight and would soon do something about it and that we were to keep the faith." They returned home feeling hopeful but again nothing happened. A second letter was sent by Kieran on 27 September 1983, three months after the first.

Your Excellency,

On behalf of our Committee, I wish to inform you that we are appalled and seriously concerned at the apparent lack of interest in the continuing problems in the Poulfur curacy, parish of Templetown.

We are surprised that no acknowledgement has so far been received in respect of our letter dated 25th July, which was sent by registered post.

We trust that some corrective action can soon be taken,

Anxiously awaiting your reply

Sincerely yours,

This time a reply was received in a letter dated 3 October 1983.

I wish to acknowledge receipt of your letters of September 27th and July 25th concerning the Parish of Templetown. The reason that you did not receive a reply to your first letter is due to the fact that I was aware of the fact that you had also written to his Eminence Cardinal O'Fiaich about your problem. In any case I can assure you that

66

the area of concern is being considered carefully by the Holy See.

With my kind personal regards and prayerful good wishes, I remain,

Devotedly yours in Christ,
Gaetano Alibrandi,
Apostolic Nuncio

Despite this careful consideration by the Holy See, there was no change in the situation in Fethard. Áine, Kieran's wife, says they watched with mounting horror as Fortune's control of the parish continued, seemingly unchecked. "We were unlucky with our clergy on a number of occasions," says Kieran, "but this one beat all. We felt that after all our efforts nothing had been done."

Fortune continued to abuse. On one occasion he organised a retreat in Loftus Hall, a convent run by the Rosminian Sisters, which was located on the tip of the Hook Peninsula. It is remembered locally how quiet and secretive the youngsters were when they returned, refusing to tell parents what went on. Some have never spoken about it, but those that eventually did share what went on spoke of Fr Fortune's encouraging a naked pillow fight and talking to the young boys individually about sex. Had they ever seen a boy naked? Had they ever felt close to a boy?

At least one boy, Maurice (not his real name), was abused when Fr Fortune took him into his room. Maurice was made to masturbate Fr Fortune and then the priest attempted to do the same to him. However Maurice was pre-pubertal at the time and did not get an erection. Afterwards Fr Fortune warned him to keep quiet.

"Don't tell anyone," he said to Maurice, as he allowed him back to the dormitory with the other boys. "Tell them we had a bet that you wouldn't spend the night in [a room known as] the Devil's Room."

It was the first of many episodes of abuse which Maurice had to endure. They occurred mainly at the priest's home under the guise of Maurice's receiving grinds. On another occasion he remembers it happening after the priest had attended a family dinner at his home. Fr Fortune had offered a lift to Maurice's brother, who was travelling to another part of the county. On the way home he abused Maurice who remembers that afterwards Fr Fortune stopped to pick up a public address system.

Some time later Maurice told Fr Fortune that he had had a chat with his father about sex and homosexuality. His dad had said that homosexuality was wrong. "Have you told him?" asked Fr Fortune.

"Not yet," replied Maurice.

Fr Fortune told Maurice that what had occurred between them was not wrong, that because he was a priest he could not get married. "It will be our secret."

Maurice told no one of these incidents because he thought no one would believe him. His parents were very religious. He knew it was wrong but had no idea at that time that it was a criminal offence. Afterwards he felt confused and guilty.

Fourteen-year-old Colm O'Gorman met Fr Fortune when the priest introduced himself to him at a workshop for religious groups he was attending in Enniscorthy. A few weeks later, Colm remembers the priest turned up unannounced at his home in Wexford to discuss folk groups and "liturgical mime" with him. During that conversation, he began talking about sex and asked Colm if he masturbated. Before he left, Fr Fortune invited him to Poulfur for a weekend. However, he explained, there was only one bed and they would have to share it. That Friday evening Fr Fortune turned up to collect him. That night when they both went to bed Colm could hardly believe it when the priest took off both their pajamas and began to abuse him. Afterwards Colm got dressed and went down to the kitchen. He felt horrible. He felt guilty and responsible. He told Fr Fortune it was wrong and could never happen again. Fr Fortune agreed.

The next day, on the way home, Fr Fortune told Colm he was worried about him and said that he needed help. To receive that help he would have to come down to Poulfur again. If he did not do this, Fr Fortune would have to tell his parents. Colm recalls feeling trapped, that there was no way out and he was damned.

"After that first time, he blackmailed me into going back. I was very shocked and felt guilty, and it triggered a lot of stuff because I had been abused before. When I think of it now, I want to go back eighteen years and grab myself out of that car and say, 'No, it's not your fault.'"

The abuse continued for around two and a half years. Colm would be brought from Wexford to the parochial house at weekends. One summer he spent a few weeks at the house. On one of those nights, he was buggered by Fr Fortune. The abuse always occurred in Poulfur except for one occasion in late 1983 when Fr Fortune called to his house in Wexford and abused him after Colm's father had gone to bed. It was the last time it was to happen.

Colm left school that year. As a summer project he opened a coffee shop. The venture was not a success and he was in debt. He went to Fr Fortune for help. In response he said he would give him £300, but only if Colm were to find another boy for him to sleep with, his own age or younger. Colm refused. "It was the last time I saw Fr Fortune."

In the summer of 1982 another boy, sixteen-year-old Ian (not his real name), had come to Fr Fortune's attention. He was in the area on holidays with his family. The priest offered him the job of painting the outside of the parish house. Ian jumped at the opportunity because it meant he could stay longer. Matters were made easier because Fr Fortune had also offered him lodgings.

A few days after he moved in, Fr Fortune asked him to move from the spare room because it was being decorated for visitors that he was expecting. There was a spare bed in his room and Ian could sleep there. That night Ian took the smaller bed, but Fr Fortune told him to move to the bigger one where he would be more comfortable. They switched beds, but after a few minutes the priest returned to the bigger bed. He began to cuddle Ian and his hand moved down to Ian's genitals. It got progressively worse. Ian froze in the bed and pretended to be asleep. Afterwards he was terrified and lay awake all night, afraid it would begin again.

In the morning, when Fortune left to say mass, Ian packed his suitcase and travelled to the home of the family he had stayed with on his holidays. Just as he arrived there, Fr Fortune pulled up in his car. Ian dropped everything and ran to one of the toilets and tried to lock himself in, but Fr Fortune beat him to it and blocked him from closing the door. He persuaded Ian to come back to the house to "talk matters through" so that they would both have "peace of mind". He promised there would be a cleaner at the parish house. Ian remembers crying. Exhausted from lack of sleep and the effort of running away, he agreed.

Back at the house Fr Fortune said it had all been a mistake. He thought, he said, that Ian had wanted it to happen. "Think of the trouble it would cause if people found out," he said. Ian was made swear on the Bible that he would not tell anybody about it. In the end, he stayed in Fr Fortune's house for a further week before being collected by his parents, and no further incident occurred.

One of Fortune's main parish-based activities was a group called the "Family League Movement" which involved his visiting houses throughout the parish to say mass. During a sermon in one house, he astonished people by saying he had recently brought a young girl from the parish, who was attending school in a nearby town, to an

STD clinic in Dublin. A father of one of the small group of girls who did attend that particular school was very angry.

"He had narrowed it down to about six girls who were going to school in that town. A neighbour contacted us and told us. Of course we were very upset. I tried to talk to him about it but got no satisfaction."

The same man was concerned to hear that Fr Fortune had shown his Don Bosco Youth Club group the film *The Life of Brian* one Good Friday, at a time when it had been denounced by the Catholic Church and banned from Irish cinemas. When he tried to complain Fortune slammed down the telephone.

"We now know that he used to show *The Omen* and other movies like that. He never consulted the parents about what he was showing. It was his horrible way of softening up the kids for what he wanted to do to them," says the man sadly.

He and his wife decided to go and see Bishop Brendan Comiskey, who was by then the Bishop of Ferns.

"I was concerned as my children had seen the video and what effect it might have had on them, going by what Rome had said. They had denounced the film and that was enough for me."

The man says that he asked the bishop to send someone into the parish to investigate, but was never aware of it if such an investigation were carried out. He felt that this approach, and others made over the years to people in authority, had come to naught.

Chapter 6

"Enthusiasm, Zeal and Love"

Sᴇᴀɴ Cʟᴏɴᴇʏ ᴄᴏɴᴛɪɴᴜᴇᴅ to watch the curate closely. "He was the greatest liar that I ever met, a horrible man. He had all the deadly sins except sloth."

Kathleen (not her real name) still shudders, almost twenty years later, remembering her experience when she found herself at the receiving end of Fortune's wrath. Kathleen is an older sister of Jim, the boy whom Fortune abused one night when he asked him to stay over at his house because of the bad weather.

Kathleen, who had been told of the abuse by her sister Angela, was determined that Fortune would not baptise her child, who was born in December 1982. The priest visited her in the hospital and mentioned the christening, but rather than challenge him there, she decided that she was simply going to go to Canon Mernagh and ask him to christen her little girl.

Despite the years that have passed, Kathleen has a vivid memory of Fortune's calling to her home in Poulfur to make arrangements for the christening. When she told him that she did not want him to perform the ceremony, he told her she and the baby would be cursed with bad luck.

"I remember it was a freezing cold day, a Friday morning. I had the floor in the kitchen half swept. There was music on the radio and I was dancing with my other two little ones, who were toddlers. We were playing ring-a-ring-a-rosy. The baby was in the pram on one side of the room. She was just nine days old. Fortune would never knock or anything and he was in the kitchen before I knew where I was.

"The baby was in the pram on one side of the kitchen and we were on the other. He stood right beside the pram and asked me about the christening. I told him I didn't want him to do it. He started shouting at me over the pram that I couldn't get another priest without his consent. At that time I knew no different, but I insisted that it would not be him. Then he told me that I would have no luck and she would have no luck. He said he would talk about it from the altar. I can remember it so well. I was very frightened and we had no telephone in the house then and my husband was out at work. I was hysterical that day after it. Even today if my daughter gets sick, I think of it and worry and would nearly start crying. I was terrified when she got convulsions when she was small."

Kathleen's husband told Canon Mernagh what had occurred and he said the couple should bring the baby to the church in Templetown that Sunday and have her baptised. "It was all done in such a hurry the poor little thing didn't even have a godmother. The christening cake was still in the freezer," recalls Kathleen.

Word of the episode spread, and one day around a year and a half later, Kathleen remembers, Sean Cloney told her that he and another man were going to talk to the newly arrived Bishop Comiskey about Fortune and asked if she wanted to complain about her episode. As far as she remembers, the two men wanted to speak to the bishop about the row over the community hall.

"We went in and I told Bishop Comiskey the story. He said that he knew all about it already. He said he hadn't met Fortune but that something would be done about him in a few weeks. I didn't mention the episode with Jim and what had happened to him at that stage. I will always carry the guilt for that with me. I didn't know then that there were others as well as him. I thought the bishop was a very nice man and that we were on to a winner. I remember thinking, 'This is it; he will really slaughter the other fella.' It was so hard having him here as a priest for those years after. Every day when you would go up to the school, he would be there. But it just felt like nobody wanted to listen to us or wanted to know about it. It was like he was leading his own cult; he was the ruler and that was it, and his main interest was getting money from people. I know a woman who was involved with the credit union. He wanted the money from her and when she refused Fortune told her that he would have her child taken from her. I'm convinced that he was evil."

Sean Cloney also remembered that Bishop Comiskey said at that meeting he would take some action against Fortune within three weeks. "As far as we were concerned, we could see no evidence of that. Of course, it was very disappointing. We felt we had no success with Bishop Herlihy either. He said, 'What can I do with him?' He felt powerless. But now we had a new bishop, a virile young man. But it seemed like we had no more luck. Years went by and it seemed like nothing was being done."

Sean assisted another local woman in writing a letter to Dr Comiskey after Fortune told her that her son would not be confirmed unless he had enough points built up. The only way of building up these points was for the boy to join the various organisations run by the priest. The bishop, according to Sean, responded to the letter, stating that there was no such requirement.

One day in 1984 a friend of Kieran and Áine's, a priest based in the UK, arrived at their home in Fethard. After a while the conversation turned to Fr Fortune, and they explained their various efforts to have something done about the curate. After hearing their tale, the cleric encouraged the couple to write a letter to Bishop Comiskey. Like Sean Cloney, this man felt that with a new bishop there was an excellent chance that some action would be taken. They decided to give it one last shot. Áine sat down and with Kieran's help she wrote a letter. The date on their copy of that letter is now illegible, but the couple believe it would have been sent some months after the bishop arrived in April that year.

Dear Bishop Comiskey,

This visit is to appraise you of the situation in the curacy of Poulfur which has been continuing and escalating since July 1981. Basically the issues concern extraordinary behaviour and pastoral scandal which are brought to your attention in the hope that a just, remedial solution might be found before deterioration broadens the scandal and divisions.

We attach for greater wholeness and at your convenience a resume of points made to your late Predecessor, whose death postponed the enquiry and action urgently sought. On all items submitted we are prepared to substantiate fully information necessary and sufficient to establish the whole truth.

The letter went on to appeal to the bishop to hold a thorough inquiry, "in the loyal hope that the Gospel will be upheld and peaceful relationships be enabled to grow and develop". Attached to the letter were a number of points concerning Fr Fortune, as well as details of representations made to others in the Catholic Church. This document was drawn up and set out with reference to canon law and the grounds on which the couple believed the bishop could take action:

These communications express serious concern and the background to the present situation.
–This is to ask you for an enquiry into longstanding grievances covering a period of years.
–Present state: Faith, Morals, Justice and Scandal.

A Message from Heaven

Scandal: Priesthood, Ministry and Sacraments are brought into disrepute and odium through
1 Violations of confidentiality.
2 Defamation and division by calumny and detraction. Gossip–Hearsay communicated in a vindictive spirit in the community.
3 Authoritarian actions and disregard for the rights, dignity and interests of the community (self-interest).
4 Adverse influence on Youth and Family Relationships.
5 Questions of Accountability – especially financial.
6 (Church & Station mass) Eucharist to non-Catholics.
7 Unnecessary innovation and Dubious Ecumenism.
8 Commercialisation of the Sacraments and the Priest's role.

A1 Violations of Confidentiality, serious indiscretion:
–To a group of twenty mothers a statement was made "that seven local youths are now expectant single parents".
–After a shop break-in witnesses were told the identity of the offender was known through the confessional. The identity was not revealed but the statement caused scandal to the witnesses.

A2 Defamation and Division by Calumny and detraction— Gossip—Hearsay Communicated in a vindictive spirit in the community.
–From the altar personal attacks aimed at recognisable figures and groups.
–At a hotel function, before a mixed group the statement was witnessed that "all first-born of Macra should be crippled"—this is on affidavit.
–After going to the aid of a lightening victim, A. [Áine] was herself injured requiring 8 stitches. On hearing this SF [Fortune] stated "she didn't get half enough".
–Macra is a bad organisation and no parent should allow their children to join.

A3 Authoritarian actions and disregard for the rights, dignity and interests of the community (self interest).

–Personal control of 34 clubs and organisations.

–Occasion of Dr Herlihy lying in state. Easter '83, "Satan would haunt the organisers of the hall disco function" (reference to Hall committee who had been authorised to continue the function by Parish priest Canon Mernagh).

–Personal threats: isolation of Pioneer Total Abstinence members who legally tried to raise funds. These members were supported by the PP Canon Mernagh.

Recent example August 1, 1984 – MM told by SF that the objectors to his house building were K and A [Kieran and Áine]. This was false gossip. Confronted over this at a meeting between MM, SF and A to establish the truth, explain and apologise the reaction was extraordinary – no retraction. Instead effort was made to eject the victim of defamation by calling the police. This behaviour is frequent it seems whenever SF is challenged to substantiate his broadcast information.

–Infiltration (through caucus), and undermining of several community groups or organisations and the setting up of alternative, rival dubious organisations, totally subservient to SF's personal dictatorship – publicly admitted – e.g. Spurious hall committee, lockout etc – allegedly with the Bishop's approval – subsequently proven false but never retracted.

Threats have been made to expectant mothers (affidavit available). One example ". . . your child will be born handicapped . . ." (if child to be christened by PP).

A4 Adverse influence on Youth and family Relationships:
 –Beach Party (14–18 year olds). This was supposed to be under clerical supervision. In the event it was not so supervised. Lasted until 4 a.m. and alcohol, drugs, contraceptives were in use.

–Following this SF arranged for police to raid and stop a supervised ceili for adults at 12.30 a.m. . . . This was reprisal and vindictive action.

–Loftus Hall Weekend Retreat for youth, 12 January 1982,

for over 15s. The weekend was repeated and in all about sixty youths attended. Participants were instructed not to disclose the nature of and content of the retreat even to their parents. It is believed intimate sexual matters were on the agenda.

–Video "nasties" – "The Exorcist", shown mid-Lent, "The Life of Brian" shown Good Friday, both examples would seem inappropriate for both age-range and times shown (14-16 year olds).

A5 *Questions of Accountability – especially financial:*
–Money talk, sources of revenue, (Parochial), Curacy overdraft.

–Pioneer Total Abstinence Association works on Goodwill, they are not fund raising without rights. Exclusive rights are claimed to dispose of funds.

–Misuse of parochial funds e.g. secret draws, no winners' lists made public.

A6 *Eucharist to non-Catholics.*

A7 *Financially motivated performances, showmanship:*
Baptisms, Weddings, House Masses, Site Blessings, Boat blessings, blessing of monuments, memorials, even "fun and games" centre, despite having earlier orchestrated and actually assisted in a Court objection to the licence application. It is remarkable who now contributes to sponsorship of programmes.

–Processions, Faith-healing, patrons, Harvest Thanksgiving.

A8 *Abuse of State Funds:*
–Youth employment schemes, supervision of participating youths re conditions of employment etc. Blatant manipulation of funds and personnel.

–T.V. Mass reportedly yielded £600 last year, hence the much-advertised encore?

–Special local newspaper column, Poulfur notes, promotes all his own activities and those of his financial supporters to the exclusion of competing events.

–Newsletters, Showcards, Parochial Secretary and Office equipments.
–Division is being created among people while investigation, enquiry and the "whole truth" is not sought.
–This approach to the Bishop is made in the interests of truth, charity, and justice for the good of the whole community.
–Neglected or delayed inquiry condones the injustice and scandal – counter testimonials being solicited [by Fortune].

As it turned out, Kieran and Áine also felt their optimism in the new bishop was misplaced: "He didn't even acknowledge our letter. As a follow up, we made an appointment to see him. I think it was his birthday because we brought him in a salmon. We told him of our fears and worries that the parish was crumbling. We told him how manipulative Fortune was and that the parish was split down the middle. We did not know about the sexual abuse at that time. The bishop asked was there any suggestion in the parish that Fortune had homosexual tendencies. We told him that we had no children involved in any organisation run by Fortune but that it had been suggested locally that he was homosexual." The couple said they were not aware of any action being taken against Fortune following their complaints and they felt very disappointed. "We just stood back from it and looked after our kids. We know now that various other people went over the years for other issues," says Kieran.

Bishop Comiskey was able to judge the situation for himself in July 1985 when he visited Fethard. A photograph of a smiling Bishop Comiskey featured on the front of one of the parish newsletters announcing the visit. Parishioners were informed that the bishop was in the area for two days to meet with the pastoral council, the finance committee, the Poulfur youth club, and later to attend a celebration meal, followed by a parish dance. The next day the bishop was to concelebrate three masses in St Aidan's – the choir mass, the song mass and the folk mass.

In September of that year he returned to officially open the Poulfur Youth Employment Scheme. Those present at the opening heard the bishop describe Fr Fortune as the "Monsignor Horan of the south-east", a reference to the charismatic priest who was responsible for the building of Knock Airport.

"A great tribute is due to Fr Fortune for his efforts in securing this scheme for the area. He went out and put a tremendous amount of effort into the project," said the bishop, whose praise for the curate was reported in the local newspaper. He went on to say that during a visit to an elderly priest recently he had wondered why there had been no moving statutes in Poulfur. The priest had been told jokingly that "only one miracle is allowed per parish".

At the same event, Deputy Hugh Byrne said that in the previous eighteen months the Fethard area had lost eight young people through emigration. He congratulated Fr Fortune in securing the scheme and employment for nineteen young people in the parish. He recalled that a previous curate in Poulfur had spoken of the need for an industry in the area. "Well, we didn't get our industry, but we got Fr Fortune."

The priest's efforts to raise funds and bring employment to the area also earned him the tag "the priest with the Midas touch". It was reported that he had plans to establish an Anglo-Irish Peace and Reconciliation Centre at nearby Baginbun. Fr Fortune was quoted as saying that he wanted the centre to "transcend any North/South political or religious differences". Baginbun, the site of the first Norman landing in Ireland, "would be an appropriate location for such a centre in the Republic".

The *Sunday Press* reported that a priest known as "Fr Goldfinger" and "King Midas" had managed to "wrestle £4 million in as many years from the Exchequer for projects in the village of Fethard-on-Sea", including a day-care centre for the elderly, a nursery school "for deprived children between the ages of three and four and a half", and a twenty-four-hour emergency counselling service.

As time went on, however, the articles also began to tag the word "controversial" before his name.

Fortune would trumpet the schemes as his finest contribution to the area and, indeed, there was work done, but look around Fethard today and there is little to show for all the money that was supposed to have been allocated and spent, despite all of Fortune's boasts. Anything that is still visible is tainted by his memory. At the time any criticisms or suspicions about the schemes were quelled by the fact that he also would arrange work to be done on private houses. "All projects will be considered that will be of benefit to any particular person or persons in the local community."

Each week Fortune would dock £5, and sometimes £10, per week from the wages of those working on the schemes. They were told that the money was needed for administration and were required to hand back the amount to the priest after they had cashed their cheques. At any one time there could be up to thirty-six people involved in a scheme. The priest was also handling the grants provided for materials.

One of the ANCO schemes he set up was called "Nightwatch" and involved young men patrolling the roads of the area at night. "We were on night duty," explains one man, Gerry (not his real name), who was part of the scheme. "We would go around to old people in their homes and stay up all night cycling around the parish." The same man was also involved in an archaeological dig as part of a scheme.

Hugh Byrne says he went to ANCO to make a complaint concerning the siphoning of funds which was quickly becoming the stuff of local legend. "I made a complaint, but they were afraid of him. As the years went on, I think they did begin to restrict things, but they were intimidated."

However, the deputy points out that he only heard about the allegations of sexual abuse around six months before the priest left the parish in 1987. He had been involved in organising a number of deputations to Bishop Comiskey in an effort to get something done about other matters. Byrne says that when the deputations returned they had told him that the bishop had said "it would be sorted" but that they had never seen any evidence of anything happening.

"I organised deputations to go in. I don't know if the bishop was afraid of Fortune, like so many other people were. The bishop always seemed to have more time for the younger priests, and it seemed as if Fortune was a friend of his."

Billy Moroney had kept in touch with events in Fethard since the abortion referendum in 1983. A member of the Labour Party at that time, he says he spoke to senior people within the party about the money being taken by Fortune from people doing community employment schemes.

"I felt that what he was doing was illegal and wrong. I told lots of people but no one was prepared to listen. In the mean time, things were just getting worse in Fethard. As time went on I heard about the visits to the bishop and to Monsignor Shiggins and the papal nuncio. It was a terrible thing to have a churchman in that position, creating such a divide in the community. After a while the surrounding parishes began to get sucked into it – people began either travelling great distances to go to Fr Fortune's mass or great distances to get away from it. You can imagine the kind of hassle it all caused in rural Ireland of that time. Of course, matters were greatly exacerbated by the history of Fethard. The fact that the Cloneys were at the centre of things that had happened before and that they were now standing up to Fortune caused problems. People, including those in the Church, seemed to put it down to them causing problems, and that apparently meant that they were not prepared to examine the issues. If there was never a child abused, there was enough trouble and torment and strife and rumours about money; abuses in employment schemes; people being conned out of their money; phoney healing. There was more than enough of all that going around for an investigation to be held. But it seemed to me as if they may have just decided it was Sean Cloney getting his revenge. I remember that other priests used to talk about Fortune, and joke with grumbling parishioners that weren't they lucky they didn't have to put up with Fortune. He was regarded as somewhat of a joke. But then sometime in the mid-1980s that stopped. I think that's when they knew there were more serious goings on. But we saw no sign of an investigation. The Church and state seemed to be turning a blind eye to some terrible things."

Indeed terrible things continued to happen. Fr Fortune continued to corner young boys in what was by now a sickeningly familiar manner. He would ask questions about their burgeoning sexuality and any homosexual inclinations they may have had.

"I'll give you £20 for a blow," he told a fourteen-year old boy.

"You can have anything you want if you go to bed with me," he said to another teenager.

On one occasion a young boy who had been called out of the youth club meeting by the priest came back after a time and told the others he had "thumped" Fr Fortune. Money was pressed on those he had imposed upon, a non-too-subtle bribe to keep quiet. Most were afraid to report him, and some did not realise what he had done to them was a crime. Others felt their parents would not believe them. In such a small community, the shame would be dreadful.

Fortune's abuse of his parishioners, both sexual and otherwise, became the subject of an anonymous poem, which was circulated to the diocese in the late 1980s.

A Message from Heaven

The poem, entitled "Thoughts after the Hunt, or Smell-egy in a Country Churchyard (with apologies to Shaw and Gray)", included a preface:

> The unspeakable in pursuit of the uneatable
> Were abused by one most hypocritical
> Hounds under the bridge, where grave sacrilege,
> And much more that was quite unrepeatable.

It went on:

> Yes, I tar with some brush all who dabble in slush
> Give support, or consent with their silence
> To an unprincipled cur with a collar, non-fur,
> Though some suggest others use violence.

> With a nod and a wink, they've kept covered with a stink
> That was never a subject for banter,
> While our parish is split by this foul hypocrite,
> This rude, semi-literate ranter.

> Take the lid off the can, crozier-carrying man
> Of God, as you value hereafter,
> It's with you the buck stops, in your court the ball hops.
> Rip the collar from off this imposter.

The concluding verse read:

> Did you come and to make our hearts burn,
> Or to nod and to smile, and to pat on the hair
> Then let us go home with an inner despair
> Nor restore us to our faith as we hope you might do,
> Nor prove a true shepherd, so long overdue?

Finally in 1987 it was announced that Fr Fortune was leaving Fethard. He did still have many supporters, and at the end of September a few hundred people gathered for his going-away party at a local hotel. A letter from Dr Comiskey paying tribute to the curate for his "enthusiasm, zeal and love" was read out. The priest told those gathered that he left behind many happy memories but had requested a transfer since he had achieved many of his goals in six years spent there. The then thirty-three-year-old curate said he was moving to London to do a media course and to assist in the work of a newly formed parish in Acton. After being presented with a crystal lamp by the Poulfur Pastoral Council, he told the gathering that it was not the only thing he would be taking with him: now standing at seventeen stone, he said he had accumulated a stone in weight for each of the six years he had been in the curacy.

Afterwards he would tell people that the climate in Fethard meant that his enthusiasm for change had annoyed people. His aim had been to bring people together, mainly through his ecumenical services. Somewhat ironically, he said Sean Cloney had disagreed with this and together with some other local people begun to make complaints against him. In all, though, he said, he spent "six fairly happy years in the parish organising local employment schemes, renovating schools, halls, churches, the parochial house etc."

Fr Fortune left many unpaid bills behind him in Fethard, with some estimates amounting to thousands of pounds. According to Kieran and Áine, he burnt almost everything relating to the parish's financial affairs before his departure. The few account books that remained were covered in white corrector fluid, blanking out various transactions. The couple says that when Dr Comiskey sent diocesan financial controller Michael Murray, now deceased, to the parish, he told them that having looked through the house there was nothing for him to work on. All he could do was to take charge of clearing the bills.

"He told us that when he went to the priest's house he had destroyed almost every shred of evidence. He even took the light bulbs out of the house. All the computers and everything were gone," said Áine.

Fr Sean Fortune had come to the parish virtually penniless, but by the time he left he had all the appearances of someone who had amassed a considerable amount of money. Besides what he had siphoned from the community employment schemes, as well as the other grant aid he had managed to bring in, there was the money from the insurance settlements from the various car accidents, as well as the proceeds from his "healing" masses which attracted people from all over the county and beyond.

"I remember a fella who broke his back, a young man in the prime of his life. He was paralysed after an accident," says a local man. "For months after that Fortune was saying masses for him at a fee. He promised him that he would get him to walk. There was another woman that he 'cured'; of course she was dead not long after. It would sicken you to watch it."

Following Fr Fortune's departure, the *New Ross Standard* wrote of the curate who had had an "uncanny ability" to secure state aid and who had created more than seventy jobs and secured close to £1 million in state grants for the area. The priest was no stranger to controversy, stated the article; he had left behind "a rich legacy of job creation, social, pastoral and ecumenical achievement, but also a community deeply divided".

Fr Sean Devereux (in Wexford the x is pronounced) was sent to Poulfur to replace Sean Fortune. It was the first parish appointment for the good-looking young priest. Fr Devereux was also interested in young people, but this was an entirely different interest from the one shown by his predecessor, and parishioners slowly began to breathe a sigh of relief. Still, even then, it seemed a strange decision to send such a young, inexperienced priest to clear up the unholy mess created by the previous incumbent.

While Fortune may have left Fethard considerably richer than when he arrived, the same could not be said for the parish coffers. Shortly after his arrival Fr Devereux told mass-goers that the Poulfur curacy was in debt. According to a newspaper report at the time, the curacy, which had won £250,000 in state grants towards job creation, had itself fallen into a deficit of £15,700.

Fr Devereux, quoted in the piece about the debt, denied that there was any impropriety connected with the ANCO schemes. According to the report Fr Devereux, who was being assisted in managing the finances of his first curacy appointment by the office of Bishop Comiskey, had explained that parish accounts were completely separate from state funding received for job creation in the area.

"The deficit has nothing to do with Department of Labour and Manpower schemes which were absolutely in order," said the priest. The curacy was in the red because of extensive renovations at St Aidan's Church and Poulfur parochial house and office over recent years. "While Fr Devereux could not comment on reports locally that the curacy had been in the black some years ago, he confirmed that considerable work had been carried out on the house in recent years," stated the newspaper.

That work had included restoration of the cellars of the parochial house, some reroofing and new windows and doors. The curacy, Fr Devereux explained, had taken out a term loan for £11,000 to finance the building and restoration work, so the actual debt stood at an overdraft of £4,000. "The people of Poulfur curacy have been working to clear off the term loan and they are also willing to clear off the overdraft."

The finances of the curacy were not all that Fr Devereux had to deal with in Poulfur. His affinity with young people meant that they soon began to trust him. One of those who became friendly with the new priest was Paul Molloy. Paul remembers well that summer of 1987 when Fr Fortune was taken out of the parish and replaced by Fr Devereux. As an assistant leader of the youth club, he had a meeting with him one day and soon the talk turned to Fr Fortune. It was the first of several discussions, and Paul eventually revealed to the priest what had happened to him.

"He started asking questions about Fr Fortune. In a roundabout way, he said he was sent to clean up the mess. In the end he was only left in Poulfur for a year and a half. I think that I gave him a little more than he bargained for. He met with me regularly for about a two-week period. I could see that he was sincere, but that he may have found the stuff about Fortune a little hard to believe. He told me that I had two options: I could take the case to the Church or to the gardaí, but that if I did that, and there was a case, my name could come out. I don't know if that was deliberate or that I misunderstood him . . . Of all the priests that I came across, he was the most honest. At seventeen my main concern was that it would be kept quiet. He recommended that I write a brief letter about it to the bishop. Then he asked me if I would be free on Saturday [4 November 1988]. I told him that I would be and on that day he brought me to All-Hallows in Dublin. When we got there, we met another priest and he asked me a few questions, I don't think in any great detail. He gave me some foolscap paper and a pen, and he asked me to write down everything that had happened with Fortune. He left me sitting in a room for a few hours and came and checked on me a while later. Once I finished writing that was the end of it. I wonder now why it was held outside of the diocese. As far as I know, under canon law, the bishop could have appointed someone within the diocese, but we still went to All Hallows, which I think was very strange."

Paul was never told at that time what Fortune's part was in this process or whether he had even been informed that it was going on. However, he is now aware that the priest was interviewed but believes this interview took place some months after his own. Paul suspects that Fortune may have been provided with a list of questions in advance, perhaps have even seen Paul's statement. Fr Devereux declined to be interviewed for this book.

"I don't know how the bishop looked on this whole thing because I was never told," says Paul. "I never heard another word about this as to the outcome of it, whatever you want to call it, this process, because it was never formally named. There was a suggestion made to me by Fr Devereux that there should be some form of inquiry or tribunal. I did get a letter from Bishop Comiskey after All Hallows. It was such a long time ago now that I don't remember the exact wording. I know it has been said that he apologised – he didn't – but he spoke about things like 'your time of trouble' and that he was 'sorry about the matter at hand'. The letter was stored away at home for a number of years, but my mother, in a fit of annoyance one day, tore it up. Back then I was so disgusted with the whole thing that I just let it go. Typical of Fr Fortune, he did try and contact me again afterwards. I had gone to England at the time. He telephoned my mother looking for my address. My mother told me and I said I didn't want anything to do with him. When he called her back and she told him that I didn't want to see him, he asked her if there was a reason why."

Increasingly disenchanted, Paul moved to the US in 1989. "I was sick of the whole thing. I wanted to get out and put it all behind me."

Another boy who had been abused says he also told Fr Devereux about the incident. The priest told him the matter should be reported to Bishop Comiskey. Afterwards he heard nothing more. A local man who was friendly with Fr Devereux around this time said that as far as he could see the young priest had been sent in to "pick up the pieces".

"He told me that at one stage he was counselling six boys after what Fr Fortune had done to them. He was only left in the parish for a short time. I guess he was unearthing more than was considered wise."

In the years after his own abuse, Don spent a considerable amount of time warning people about Fortune. He continued to come across the priest at functions in Wexford, to hear him on the radio, or to see him on television.

"I have a friend who was involved in a youth group, and she told me one day that a very nice priest in Poulfur had invited her down with the group. I warned her that he had been abusing people, but she felt it was too late to back out. I ended up going out to Poulfur with them. I would have been around eighteen years old. When he saw me, he said, 'How're ya, Don?' I looked him in the eye and I said, 'I'm fine.' I think those were the only two words that I spoke to him for the weekend. I spent my time trying to keep the kids together and keep an eye on them. I wouldn't let them out of my sight. I knew they were prime meat for Johnny. I was giving rants about him for years, telling people about him. I met ten people from around the country who had direct experience of him. Two guys from Kilkenny and Waterford were hitching one day and he picked them up and tried it on with them. I know of a guy who was training to be a priest who left afterwards. He was ministering to this man who was very sick, he was dying, but all that concerned the man was that his grandson had been abused by Fortune. I met a girl from Poulfur, and when I told her about him she turned white because her brother had said it but they did not believe him. A guy from Dublin told me that he came on holidays to Poulfur and all the other kids told him to stay away from the priest."

Local traders were not the only ones left with bills after Fr Fortune's departure. Gerry, who had regularly done the collections at masses in St Aidan's and had been involved in the Nightwatch scheme, was also left out of pocket. The priest had found out that Gerry had inherited a small sum of money. He approached him one day and said he needed a new telephone system for the parochial house. He asked Gerry for a loan of £1,700, almost exactly the amount of money he had inherited.

"He got someone to bring me on my bike to get it. Later he got me when I was on my bicycle and asked me for my signature on a piece of paper which he did not let me read. Then before he left Fethard he got me to sign a second piece of paper. That day there was a builder in my house and he got him to sign it, too. Then when he went away he took all telephones with him."

Kieran and Áine explained that they have acted as guardians for Gerry for a number of years and were very concerned to hear about this money and the requests for his signature. "It turns out that the second piece of paper stated that Fortune could take the subject of the purchase for his sole use and purpose," said Kieran. "Gerry told us that he understood that it was an interest-free loan for twelve months, but he never got it back. I sent for Fortune and said we needed to have an urgent discussion about the money," said Kieran. "When he arrived I said, 'Johnny, no bloody way you are conning Gerry out of his money.'

"I told Fortune to tell Gerry why he wanted the second signature, and he said it was just to extend the loan. He wouldn't show the piece of paper, but then he admitted that it stated that he could take the telephone equipment with him. I said, 'You are some bastard. I'd swear if I lifted your cassock you would have cloved hooves.' I told him he was possessed and he just laughed at me. I told him that proved it. But then he went bananas, saying that the money was his. I told him that with interest he owed Gerry £1,900. He walked out."

Áine then telephoned Michael Murray, the diocesan financial controller. "He promised the matter would be investigated further. He told us that he had told the bishop and again we waited. Then we told the story to Fr Devereux. He said he would go into Wexford about it. Anytime I would meet Fr Devereux afterwards, I would tell him that Gerry had not yet got his money back, and he would say he was doing what he could about it. Then when Fr Joe McGrath arrived, I told him about it. One day I went with him into Bishop Comiskey and said it was shocking that someone in clerical garb would do what Fortune had done. The bishop, in fairness, agreed. He said to leave it with him and he would make sure that the cheque with interest would get to Gerry. However he couldn't say when or how."

In January 1989, two years after the money had been lent, the cheque arrived. It was handed over via Fr McGrath. "I know that some people think it is dreadful that we asked him for the money back," says Áine. "To this day they feel like that. I know of one woman and Fr Fortune is still like a son to her. She would never believe any of the stories about him."

Chapter 7

An Extraordinarily Energetic Priest

A PICTURE OF the Sacred Heart has hung on the wall of Don's family home in Wexford for many years. Recently it fell, shattering the frame. His mother Brid says that until then she had not consciously looked at it for a long time. When she picked it up she saw that the familiar holy image contained inside had remained intact. Underneath, in the space reserved for the name of the family and the papal blessing, the writing was still legible. It was the signature of a priest – Fr John Fortune. The day he had performed this consecration was the day in April 1982 when he took their son Don to Poulfur and abused him.

So many years later and they are still clearly shattered by what happened. Sitting in the living room of their home, Brid describes it as "that awful day". As Michael speaks about their experience, Brid leaves the room and returns with the picture of the Sacred Heart and the broken picture frame. She is somewhat bemused that they have left it hanging for all those years, but she also seems to realise that removing it would merely have been a cosmetic exercise. Fortune's influence on their family goes very deep. Strong Catholics, they had welcomed him into their home.

"We got the Sacred Heart from Michael's mother as a wedding present. We had it consecrated when Don and his brother were born, but it had not been signed. We would have done it again when all the family were born and we

93

had been in the house for a number of years. But he did it, and we weren't even here. He did it on the day he abducted our son."

Michael felt he had had no success when he went to complain to the late Bishop Herlihy about the abuse his son had suffered. When the new bishop, Dr Brendan Comiskey, arrived, he too decided it was a good time to make another approach to Church authorities. The couple was already greatly impressed by him.

"He came with this great aura about him, almost like a pop idol type. People were ringing me and telling me that we were very lucky to be getting such a fantastic bishop. He set the place alive. He took to the people. He was a total politician. His homilies were brilliant; you could hardly get into the church."

Michael believes that Dr Comiskey, as a new bishop, would not have been given any formal communication concerning the previous problems with Fortune or other priests who had complaints made against them prior to his appointment. "Apparently when a bishop took over all the records from the previous bishop were destroyed; they were classed as somehow being almost part of the confessional. The only details passed over were those about bursaries left to the diocese. I think Bishop Herlihy used to burn records anyway."

However, in a statement in 1996, Dr Comiskey would say that he became aware of complaints of sexual abuse against priests in the diocese, which were held on file, "almost immediately" after he arrived in Ferns in 1984. Michael says that when he met with Dr Comiskey the bishop revealed to him that he was already aware of complaints against Fortune, no doubt those from Fethard and possibly some of the earlier complaints made while Fortune was involved in the Scouts as a seminarian in St Peter's. While in Fethard they may have been unaware that their complaints had resulted in any action, in fact the bishop had listened to them and sought the advice of medical experts and other clergymen.

"When I went to speak to Bishop Comiskey about Fortune, he was already after taking him in and having him assessed," says Michael. "A number of senior parish priests were brought in to see if they could help to sort it out. I know that when the bishop questioned Fortune about the complaints, he took the Bible and swore on his priestly vows that it was all lies. You would have to have no worry about your mortal soul to do that. If you were a good priest, regardless of the weaknesses that you [Dr Comiskey] had, could you say to another priest, 'You are a terrible, complete evil, lying bastard'? The bishop has been much maligned in relation to Fortune. I know that he had deputations about Fortune's behaviour, but equally he was contacted by people who swore by him and said they would go to court and stand up for him. What did Solomon do? There was also some talk of headed notepaper being stolen and letters being written in other people's names. You would want a full-time team of investigators to keep up with Fortune. Dealing with him was like playing a game of chess, except he was always one step ahead," says Michael.

He is reluctant to elaborate on his representations to the bishop concerning the abuse of his son, except to say that it was not a matter which he forgot about. "Fortune to me had done something to my family. I was not going to forget that. I was persistent. I also knew that there were all sorts of other people trusting him and taking him into their homes."

He says Dr Comiskey had told him that he had the priest assessed twice by psychiatrists, one an eminent doctor based in London, and on both occasions he had been told that there was nothing wrong with Fortune. "The London doctor went so far as to write a letter to the bishop stating that he would be prepared to stand up in court and say this," says Michael, remembering a conversation with the bishop.

Fortune was indeed assessed in the 1980s and on a number of occasions, all during the times when he was actively abusing young boys. What was apparently his first assessment occurred shortly after his arrival in Fethard and was at the instigation of Bishop Herlihy. Fortune had been told to attend Monsignor E. Feichim O'Doherty, now deceased, who was then professor of logic and psychology at University College Dublin. Monsignor O'Doherty specialised in seeing priests with psychological problems. After this first consultation in March 1981, the situation in Fethard continued to deteriorate, and a year later Fortune was instructed by Dr Herlihy to return. The outcome of these two consultations is not known, except that as far as his parishioners were concerned he continued to wreak havoc.

In February 1985 Bishop Comiskey directed Fortune to attend Dr John Cooney, former associate medical director at St Patrick's Hospital in Dublin. In a letter to Dr Comiskey sent two years after the first appointment, the doctor wrote to "bring you up to date with the position regarding Fr Fortune". Dr Cooney would eventually recommend that Fortune should be hospitalised, but in that letter he explained that the priest had attended two appointments with a psychologist at the hospital. She had taken an in-depth case history and carried out a detailed psychological examination of him. The letter implies that the bishop had sent Fortune back to Dr Cooney in 1987 because of further complaints of sexual abuse. Dr Cooney wrote:

> She was not able to throw any extra light, so to speak, on Fr Fortune, or his problems, but is inclined to the view that he is somewhat hypomanic in temperament, as well as lacking in prudence. As far as his sexuality is concerned, she found it difficult to decide whether he was subject to the deviation which caused your Lordship to refer him back to me in the first instance.
>
> I feel at this juncture that it would be useful if I could meet with Your Lordship and discuss the matter further.

Perhaps you would be good enough to telephone me at the hospital and we could make an appointment to meet at a suitable time.

Hypomania is a medical term that describes when a person may veer between mania and depression. In the hypomanic state their mind may be over-active, with rapid change of thought processes, they may be over-talkative or have trouble speaking. It is not known if the meeting ever took place, but almost three years to the day after he had first seen Fortune and a year after the previous letter to Bishop Comiskey, Dr Cooney wrote a further report on the priest, dated 11 February 1988. At that time Fortune had left Fethard-on-Sea and was living in London, attached to Our Lady of Lourdes Church in High Street, Acton. Dr Cooney's 1988 report stated that the bishop was concerned over Fr Fortune's erratic behaviour and his failure to accept advice and guidance. He continued: "I came to the conclusion that Fr Fortune had an unstable personality and was subject to hypomanic mood swings. I discussed in detail with him the question of his sexuality, but Fr Fortune was adamant that this did not give rise to any problems whatsoever."

Fortune was also seen by another doctor at St Patrick's, who found him, according to Dr Cooney, to be "intellectually well-endowed, but confirmed my opinion of his condition".

I saw Fr Fortune on several further occasions and he professed to be following the advice which I had given him. However, I subsequently learnt from Dr Comiskey of serious allegations of homosexual practices in respect of young boys made against Fr Fortune. When I taxed him on these allegations, Fr Fortune denied these completely and was adamant that he had no difficulties in this area.

Fr Fortune's behaviour deteriorated to the extent that it was decided he should be sent for treatment to a centre in the West Midlands in the UK. With his permission in

November 1987, I sent a report to the nun in charge of the centre, Dr Breda O'Sullivan.

I subsequently saw Fr Fortune on the 31/12/87 when he assured me that all was well with him.

Subsequent reports have indicated that this man has a serious problem involving homosexual practice. Taking into account his total denial of this fact, together with his previous behaviour and his personality, I believe Fr Fortune requires a lengthy period of in-patient treatment under close supervision and that this should be instituted as a matter of urgency.

Later reports would indicate that Fortune did attend Dr O'Sullivan in Birmingham but not apparently as an in-patient; rather he travelled up from London where he was then living.

At the end of June 1988 another report was sent to Dr Comiskey. This time the assessment was arranged by Fortune and carried out by Dr Ingo Fischer, who was then director of Psychological Consultancy Service Ltd (PCS). Dr Fischer, a German who had lived in Ireland for a number of years, was a clinical psychologist. He died in 1990. Dr Fischer wrote that he had met Fortune on 21 June 1988 and carried out a series of psychometric tests. These tests measured intelligence, aptitude or emotional disturbance.

"Fr Fortune attended for assessment in order to obtain a second opinion regarding his emotional stability and other aspects of his personality about which there was some concern. These included the possibility that he is emotionally unstable, queries regarding his sexual orientation, that he may be subject to hypomanic mood swings and that he may be an alcoholic. Fr Fortune gave me a detailed account of the accusations which have been made against him over the last number of years."

In fact the test results suggested, said Dr Fischer, that the priest was a "relaxed, sociable, and emotionally stable person, who is mature, resilient and secure. He is, however, rather accommodating and not particularly assertive. This may be because of a possible need to be accepted by people and a consequent dislike and avoidance of confrontation and disagreement. Thus, it is likely that Fr Fortune will prefer to smooth things over and to compromise rather than risk upsetting someone by asserting his viewpoint. In all other respects, the report suggests that Fr Fortune is a stable person who has many positive characteristics."

Using a subsequent "personality inventory", Dr Fischer said there did not appear to be any clinical indication of emotional instability on the profile of the results.

There is a suggestion that Fr Fortune is somewhat defensive at the moment. This is, however, understandable in view of his present circumstances and the pressure which he is experiencing at the moment. Only one of his scores on this test is in any way significant. This is on a measure of concern about his health. From my discussions with Fr Fortune, he does not appear to be overly concerned about his health and, if there are any concerns, these do not appear to interfere with his effectiveness in his work or with his overall adjustment. His score on a measure of impulsivity is just reaching the significance level. These two scores together are a rather unusual configuration and one which is not typically found in a clinical population. For this reason, they would not be a particular source for us other than to suggest that Fr Fortune may tend to be somewhat impulsive and at times concerned with his health.

There is no indication of hypomanic mood swings on the test. Fr Fortune's score on the measure of hypomania is within the normal range.

As regard the question of his sexual orientation, it is difficult to assess, on the basis of a test, whether or not a person is homosexual. The test does suggest, however, that Fr Fortune's sexual orientation seems to be heterosexual and not homosexual. Again, as regard the likelihood of Fr Fortune being an alcoholic, it is not possible to state definitely whether or not this is the case here. Indeed, our understanding is that Fr Fortune is a pioneer and has never been a drinker. Our view from the test results is that Fr Fortune is no more prone to developing alcoholism than the average person. Thus, we would not have any undue concern in this regard.

The test results suggest that Fr Fortune tends to present himself in a self-righteous way. He may also be somewhat sanctimonious with regard to his value systems which, the results suggest, may in themselves be over-idealised. Thus, he may impress as being rather full of himself.

Dr Fischer went on to state that based on the assessment PCS felt that Fr Fortune should be capable of carrying out his parish, pastoral and education work in a competent manner. "In conclusion, on the basis of the test results our view is that several of the concerns expressed with respect to Fr Fortune are not supported by the evidence we have gathered. It remains, however, that there are certain aspects of Fr Fortune's personality which need to be addressed and developed."

These included his over-concern with being accepted and approved by people. This affected his ability to assert himself, which caused him to avoid confrontation even when it was warranted. "Consequently, he tends to be too accommodating of the wishes of others." The report also raised the question of Fortune's understanding of Christianity and values. "We feel that Fr Fortune needs to analyse his value systems and to clarify what these mean to him, in assessing how realistic or how idealistic they may be." Finally, the report addressed his tendency to be impulsive and to present his ideas in an ostentatious way, "which could possibly give people the wrong impression".

At Fortune's request PCS suggested an appropriate "personal development programme" which would meet his development needs. They included empathy, listening skills and interpersonal sensitivity; assertiveness, dominance and conformity; methods of improving self-presentation to avoid creating an impression of sanctimoniousness and ostentatious liberality. A half day was required for each session.

Looking back it would seem that the summer of 1987 was a turning point for Dr Comiskey as far as Fortune was concerned. It was then that the priest was transferred from Fethard. Although the report from Dr Cooney advising that Fortune had a "serious problem" had not yet been written, the complaints against him must have been stacking up in the bishop's office. The move to London was ostensibly to study journalism, but Fortune had been directed to attend sessions with Dr O'Sullivan, the Catholic psychologist. He obviously did not like the situation he found himself in and wanted to return to Ireland and be given his own parish. As well as Dr Fischer's report, the report from Dr J.R.W. Christie Brown, an eminent consultant psychiatrist with a practice on Harley Street in London, must have helped his cause.

This assessment was made over a three-day period in December 1988. Fortune spent a total of four hours with Dr Christie Brown. At that point he had actually returned from London to Ireland. He was now based at Holy Redeemer Church, Fairy Hill, in Bray. Dr Comiskey had appointed him director of the National Association of Community Broadcasting, where he was "on secondment" from the Diocese of Ferns. His new job involved travelling around the country helping out community radio stations. He liked this high profile position but he also wanted a parish.

In his report Dr Christie Brown said that before seeing Fortune he had corresponded with Dr Fischer and received a copy of the report which had been sent to Dr Comiskey. Dr Fischer had also sent him a letter dated 21 April 1988 from a "senior college counsellor" at Ealing College of Higher Education, where Fortune had been working while in London, and another letter "in the form of an open tes-timonial", dated 27 April 1988, from a hospital manager at Acton Hospital where Fortune had worked as chaplain. Finally Dr Christie Brown had spoken to "a colleague" of Fr Fortune, a priest based in the Ferns diocese. With the exception of that information, said Dr Christie Brown, all the information obtained for the purposes of the assess-ment came from Fr Fortune himself.

In his report, Dr Christie Brown restated the informa-tion he had received from Fortune about his background. Fortune assured him that there was no psychiatric illness in his family.

Dr Christie Brown said that he seemed to have been an extraordinarily energetic priest, starting thirty projects in the Fethard area. He also shared with the psychiatrist his interest in the media and his radio and television appear-ances, which he had continued while in London, con-tributing to the *Wexford Echo* and the *London Irish News.*

Dr Christie Brown spoke about letters of complaint, which he had not seen, which were written to the previous bishop (Herlihy) as soon as Fortune started in the parish. Since the present bishop took over two years later there was another rash of complaints, which then dried up.

I have not seen these letters either, nor for that matter the letters of support that Fr Fortune tells me were also sent. It appears that in 1985 there was anxiety about him. I have only Fr Fortune's account of this. He would concede that he may have been insensitive, even imprudent, in his deal-ings with people, inclined perhaps to be too forthright at some times and perhaps too familiar at others, but he would see the main reason for the complaints made against him as lying in the envy or intolerance of other people. He was asked to see Dr Cooney, a psychiatrist at St Patrick's Hospital in Dublin. Dr Cooney advised him to be more prudent and questioned him closely about the possibility that he might be homosexual. It was suggested that he should be admitted to hospital for investigation, but Fr Fortune refused this.

In June 1987, said Dr Christie Brown, Fortune had gone to London at the request of Bishop Comiskey.

> He told me that the purpose was for him to take a course at London University in Media Studies. He was also asked to go to Birmingham regularly to see Dr Breda O'Sullivan, a Catholic psychologist. The Wexford priest, to whom I spoke, indicated that the balance was the other way around. In his opinion the primary purpose of going to London was for Fr Fortune to see Dr O'Sullivan. When I subsequently took this up with Fr Fortune, he said that the primary purpose in his mind was to go on the media course but he accepted that others saw the venture differently.

In the next section the report referred to the complaints of sexual abuse which had been made the previous year by Paul Molloy. "In October 1987, a letter was sent to the Bishop from a young man of seventeen, saying that Fr Fortune had made sexual advances to him. Fr Fortune categorically denies that there is any truth in this accusation, which is now the subject of a canonical enquiry."

The report continued that while in England the priest completed his media course successfully, ran two programmes on Thamesmeade Community Radio and went to Birmingham once a fortnight to see Dr O'Sullivan. "He decided against living in a presbytery in London and rented a house instead. He had been given £6,500 for the period but because of his various expenses arranged an overdraft with the bank and is still as a result £15,000 in debt. It has subsequently been agreed that the Diocese will pay back half of this money and Fr Fortune will pay back the other half over a number of years."

Dr Christie Brown went on to say that since returning to Ireland earlier that year in May Fr Fortune had been working in the media. "He hopes for a pastoral appointment.

After his return he saw Dr O'Donohoe, a specialist in psychosexual problems at St Patrick's Hospital. I gather that he had some tests aimed at determining whether he was homosexual and there was no evidence for that," said the psychiatrist, adding that nevertheless the priest had been advised to take a drug aimed at suppressing his sexual feelings. "The arguments for this were, according to him, that he should take the drug 'in case' he might in some sense be homosexual. He says he accepted this treatment with some resentment but in obedience to the Bishop's wishes. He arranged himself an assessment with Dr Fischer, and also co-operated with the Bishop in arranging the assessment by myself."

Under the heading "alcohol history" the psychiatrist said that at the age of fourteen the priest had become a pioneer, which meant that he eschewed all alcohol. "However, he did break his pledge for a period of six months about six years ago during which time he drank one glass of wine per week."

Under the heading "sexual history" the priest had said that from the age of eleven he was aware of sexual feelings and that "before taking his vows he had a number of sexual relationships with women. All his sexual activity and sexual fantasies, including those associated with masturbation, have been of a heterosexual kind. He denies ever having had any homosexual interests or activities."

While he was at the seminary in Wexford, there was a time when there was gossip that he might have homosexual inclinations. "Subsequently, and before the written allegations, there were other occasions when there was similar gossip. Fr Fortune's view is that priests are subject to speculation about their sexual interest."

Delving into any possible history of previous psychiatric illness, Dr Christie Brown said he questioned Fr Fortune closely as to whether he had experienced periods of depression or elation in the past, or periods of disturbed sleep, increased energy, over-talkativeness and grandiose ideas. He denied any of these. He said he had received good reports from his course in London, that Dr O'Sullivan had not commented that she thought him to be ill, and that "his secretary would confirm that he had been no different from his normal self". Dr Christie Brown said he asked the Wexford priest with whom he had been in contact whether he had noticed any periods of increased excitability or depression but he said he had not.

"I note that Dr Fischer found no evidence of hypomania. I also note that Mr Jones, the hospital manager at Acton Hospital, although referring to his 'extrovert nature' had nothing but praise for him. Also, Penny Rawson, the senior college counsellor at Ealing College of Higher Education, referring to the Autumn term of 1987, writes a letter full of warm thanks."

Referring to Fr Fortune's personality, Dr Christie Brown said that the Wexford priest to whom he spoke had described him as "extremely energetic, extrovert and impetuous and certainly unrealistic about finances . . . He said that Fr Fortune always lived life at a high pitch and although he would claim to be resting at times he was never really idle at all."

Dr Christie Brown found Fr Fortune an obese man with a cheerful and direct manner. "He spoke freely, but there was no undue pressure of speech and he paused and listened appropriately. I detected no evidence for any current mental illness."

Reaching his conclusion Dr Christie Brown said it was necessary to begin with a brief account of the nature of psychiatric examination and diagnosis.

> Psychiatric diagnosis does not rely on tests which penetrate to underlying pathology in the same way as blood tests, for example, do this in physical medicine. Psychiatric diagnosis depends on detecting patterns of thought, experience and behaviour which conform to known categories of illness. If

a person suffers from an episodic illness then the presence of that illness can in no way be detected during a period of well-being between episodes. In such a situation one is entirely dependent on reliable information about the manifestations of the illness during attacks.

The detection of unusual or deviant traits of personality or character can be even more difficult than the detection of illness and this process again depends upon the gathering and sifting of evidence.

Dr Christie Brown pointed out that he had not seen the reports from Dr Cooney, Dr O'Sullivan or Dr O'Donohoe, nor did he have any further evidence as to the allegations against Fortune.

"At my examination of Fr Fortune I found no evidence of any psychiatric illness and that includes evidence of hypomania. Furthermore, I found no evidence to suggest homosexual orientation nor abuse of alcohol."

The period which caused Dr Christie Brown greatest concern was when Fortune ran up large debts in London, which could have been a manifestation of a swing into hypomania. However, he had no evidence that such a mood change did occur. The references which had been supplied to him by Fr Fortune did not suggest that he had become ill while in London. If he were to explore this further, he would need further information, including a report from Dr O'Sullivan, Fortune's course tutors and information from his secretary/housekeeper.

I have so far referred to the disorders (mental illness, homosexuality, alcoholism) which on the evidence available to me must be excluded. I turn now to give a view of Fr Fortune's personality.

His educational history indicated that he was a man of exceptional energy and enterprise.

He has many achievements to his credit and would appear to be the sort of person who can in a period of a few years do more than many of us would do in a lifetime. I can well believe that the other side of the coin of energy and achievement is that he can be irritating and can even elicit envy. On the evidence available to me my conclusion is that it is in this area of personality that the problem lies. Even though I have seen the "job description" for a curate, I cannot say that he is suitable or not suitable for such a post. It seems to me that his Bishop and his fellow clergy are in the best position to judge this point and to counsel him about it.

Dr Christie Brown advised that a decision should be taken quickly.

He recognises himself that his energy and a certain degree of impulsiveness can cause difficulty and he is happy to continue receiving counselling from Dr Fischer. I would certainly recommend that this should continue but in parallel with frank discussion between him and his superiors about his future career...

If there is any further evidence available bearing on his condition or on my conclusions, I would be happy to consider that evidence, seeing him again if necessary.

Certainly this report, coupled with the PCS report (although it is not known what the conclusions of Dr O'Sullivan in Birmingham were), must have made the situation exceptionally difficult for Bishop Comiskey as Fortune fought to be given another parish posting. An eminent psychiatrist who has read the reports says that people such as Fortune would pose a serious diagnostic challenge. They have a "remarkable ability to compartmentalise", leading double and sometimes treble lives. "When they encounter physicians, they do not stop being clever. Some of them are exceptionally wily and they know all the literature. Even in the space of the last ten years, our sensitivities and suspicions to child abusers have changed totally, and we probably err on the opposite side."

Chapter 8

Control

As you drive into the picturesque village of Ballymurn in County Wexford, the efforts of the local Tidy Towns committee are apparent in the carefully tended flowerbeds and the neat grass verges. Located off the main road between Gorey and Wexford, the village is surrounded by good agricultural land and situated near enough to Wexford to make it within easy commuting distance. The setting of the Church of the Assumption, built on a small hill in the centre of the village, makes it a popular church for weddings. It was a nice appointment for any priest.

It was here that Fr Sean Fortune made his full-time return to parish life, last experienced by him in Fethard-on-Sea, in September 1989. He had obviously won the argument with Dr Comiskey as to whether or not he should get another pastoral posting. As well as being made curate, he was also to teach religion at the Vocational School in Bridgetown, a town on the opposite side of the county.

Locals did not know very much about the new curate, although some had heard rumours of the difficulties he had caused while serving in Fethard. One Fethard man says he had read in horror of Fortune's appointment there. "First of all, there was a primary school there, and as well as that he was appointed chaplain to another school. I couldn't believe it. I spoke to a priest who was based nearby and asked him what the hell was going on. He said that giving him two schools would keep him occupied and away from 'other things' and that other priests were keeping an eye on him. I told him I thought it was nonsense. What could you do?"

Fortune began life in Ballymurn quietly enough. However, true to form he raised his own profile shortly after arriving by getting involved in local organisations, approaching all undertakings with great gusto.

One of his first tasks was to expand the parish newsletter. Besides the regular parish news, which was still included and added to, the curate also kept parishioners informed of his own activities, including his media appearances. The year he arrived in Ballymurn the four main churches had come together at the bishop's urgings to form the Christian Media Trust to make religious programmes for South East Radio. Fortune was one of the first presenters, hosting "Parish Focus".

In Ballymurn old patterns soon began to repeat themselves. People noticed that the priest was not content to be simply involved in local organisations; he wanted to be in control of them.

"He took the place by storm and wanted to get involved in everything going," recalls a Ballymurn man. "He would do huge amounts of work, but nobody could go against him. If things were not going his way, he would appoint his own people to a committee. He got into practically every organisation in the parish and tried to take it over. In the beginning he seemed a very affable bloke, but that changed. I know that people can have difficulties with individuals, but this became something else – you were either totally with him or totally against him. He was very clever at covering his tracks. If you disputed something, he would tell you that it had been said at a public meeting and was on record."

If you visit the Church of the Assumption today, the mark of Fr Sean Fortune remains. With one of his usual grandiose gestures, he insisted on the church's getting the fuller title of the Church of the Assumption and St Malachy. Inside, the building is bedecked with plaques giving the names of people who made donations for various items, including the sanctuary carpet, the refurbishment of the high altar and the candelabra, which is inscribed on the plaque as "relit by parishioners in memory of the living and the dead". The flowery phrases were always followed by the words "Blessed by Father Sean Fortune". The more obvious plaques, including one on the front of the lectern, are now covered by posters or other disguises. Some have been removed.

Upstairs in the gallery, there is what looks like a large stained glass window commemorating "The Wexford Martyrs. The Priests of 1798". Underneath the inscription is the name of the curate and also that of his bishop who gave "kind permission" for its erection. A Wexford business sponsored the "stained glass" window, which locals say they have since discovered is merely perspex.

Below this window is a large organ. The brass plaque on it says that it was "donated to Ballymurn Church by Fr Sean Fortune". When the church bells ring it is yet another reminder of him. A local man was persuaded to donate £2,000 for the automated bells, and when he later sought a receipt he was apparently told by Fr Fortune that a "cash deal" had been done and none was available.

But it is at the entrance to the church that the most poignant reminder is located. The names of Ballymurn babies who died are inscribed there on a wooden sign reading "Please pray for all who went to God at a very young age and for their parents and relatives, especially." Parents paid for the privilege of having the names of their babies included. On another occasion, he asked a local stonemason to carve the names of families buried in the graveyard on a stone plaque. The man agreed to do the work, as he had been asked, for the "benefit of the parish". Later, while carrying out the task, he discovered that those having their names carved were paying £50 each for the privilege while he was giving his services for free.

Those Fortune befriended believed he was a marvellous man. He was particularly popular with elderly people. Occasionally he would pay off debts such as outstanding ESB bills for parishioners who were down on their luck. Others who were sick seemed happy to pay the money he requested so that he could say masses for them, or money for petrol so that he could continue to visit them. Just one example is that of a local woman who had been recently widowed. He began calling to the house in the evening and she would give him a meal. The woman was lonely and still very distressed after her husband's death. When a question arose as to how she might honour his memory, what he would have wanted, Fortune suggested that she do something constructive. He suggested that she donate money towards renovations in the church. She wrote a cheque for £3,000.

The healing masses that had been so popular in Fethard were introduced at Ballymurn. People who were ill travelled in the hope that they would be made well by this priest who said he had the power of healing. "Of course, it all seems daft now, but sometimes he was so persuasive you would expect the person to get up out of the bed," says a man who remembers the services.

Around this time Fortune obviously spotted a way to combine his twin passions of media and money. He established, in 1991, the Institute of Journalism and Theatre and began offering media courses to anyone willing to pay a fee. It meant that he spent an increasing amount of time in Dublin.

Like everything else, his "institute" was mostly show and very little substance, except when he had the nous to ask people with proven journalistic records to give some lectures. The priest, who had spent less than a year studying journalism, charged students £1,000 each for four hours once a week over a twenty-five-week period. He told students he was an experienced journalist and had interviewed people such as Michael Jackson. He usually held two courses a year, renting space in RTÉ headquarters in Montrose. Courses were also run at rented rooms in UCD in Belfield for a time, and at the Jesuit-owned Milltown Institute in Sandford Road, Dublin.There were three lectures per night covering TV or radio, print journalism and public relations. There was rarely a shortage of people wanting to enrol. Sometimes he ran a shorter two-week course, charging £200, and advertised for "weekend diploma courses" in journalism, creative writing, television and radio. All profits, he said, went to Mother Theresa.

Some of the people who gave lectures were well-known Irish media figures who were experienced journalists. They included Joe Power, the then religious affairs correspondent of the *Irish Independent*, RTÉ newscaster Michael Murphy and broadcaster Liam Nolan. On one occasion, end-of-course certificates were handed out by former "Where in the World" presenter Theresa Lowe. These people had nothing to do with the running of the institute. It was not easy to turn Fortune down once he decided he would like you to lecture to his students, as was the experience of former government press secretary and broadcaster Sean Duignan. They met at a function and afterwards Fortune pestered him, telephoning and writing, until exasperated he agreed to give a lecture, simply to get rid of him.

Bil Keating, whom Fortune described as the president of the institute, worked with RTÉ as a producer until he took early retirement in 1995. He met Sean Fortune at a time when his life was not going well.

"I was very vulnerable. I had been an alcoholic and had stopped drinking, but I still had debts. During this period I became involved in the Sunday mass programme for RTÉ as director. My first assignment involved a visit to Fr Sean

Fortune in Ballymurn. When I got there, I was pleasantly surprised to find a very jolly, large man who seemed very comfortable in the world, with plenty of help. I don't particularly like priests, but he looked after us hand and foot, and that included a steak dinner.

"He was the type of person who would take your telephone number and the next thing you know there would be a box of chocolates sent. Before I knew where I was, I was being asked to present diplomas to students who had done his journalism course. I suppose I would have been brainwashed into having a respect for the clergy. I always called him Father. If I called him Sean it would have been an intimacy that I did not enjoy. The day I presented the diplomas, he gave me a cheque for £20. I was flattered and very glad of the money. A few months later I got a letter asking would I lecture. The first night I went to Jury's Hotel in Dublin – he ran classes all over the place – and afterwards I got another cheque for £20. I remember thinking it would be nice to get some sort of permanent/part-time job. I asked him why he didn't extend his school to include drama."

Fortune contacted Keating and asked him to travel to Waterford to give a lecture there. "As I entered the room he clapped his hands and said to the students, 'This is the president of the institute.' If it had been any other time or any other person, I would have said, 'What are you talking about?' Afterwards he took me out for tea and he showed me the headed notepaper with my name on it. He told me he was going to run a twenty-week drama course and a twenty-week TV course. I was thrilled to bits. I devised the drama course, and for the TV course he gave me twenty modules and told me I was to lecture on them. I looked at them and they were outrageously technical, but when I asked him about them, he was insistent. He had insinuated that his background was in television production and writing and PR, and the place that he had learned all of this was in America. I bowed to his greater knowledge. However, there was one particular module and I couldn't make head nor tail of it. I went to the RTÉ Training Centre to see if I could get some help. They were busy so I took down some books to have a look at them. I was reading one and I realised that it matched every single module in his course. I realised then why there were all these Americanisms in his notes, which I used to correct. He had indicated to all and sundry that the notes were written by him, but they were simply copied, very badly by a secretary, from the book.

"I also noticed that he was paying me disgracefully, very badly compared to the money that was coming in. Occasionally he had special guest lecturers, but when you consider he was paying me just £25 he was making a fortune. The evening that I lectured I would work for five hours. I also corrected papers, which I did meticulously. He would simply sit in the corridor and toss them off. I worked in television, so he used me as a catch to get people in. He also told them, I later discovered, that I would get them jobs. It was despicable. I used to get calls from mothers saying things like 'But what about Isabel? She was told you would make her a star.' I started taking students on visits to studios and then found out he was charging them for the visits.

"If he was afraid of a person, someone who had a strong personality, he would give them a high mark in exams. Weaker characters, and women, he gave them lower marks. My respect for him was diminishing all the time. If a student questioned the marks, he would immediately adopt a 'teacher knows best' attitude, sometimes almost on the verge of violence. This worried me, but there was nothing I could do.

"He liked to give an appearance of being important. There were electric gates at his house in Ballymurn and he had a mobile phone before anyone else did.

"At one stage he had forty-five people in one room on

a course. I reckon that the overheads must have been, at the extreme, with advertising, around £3,000, so he was getting over £40,000. He was running two courses a year, as well as the weekend courses. If anyone showed any interest he would hound them until they signed up."

The institute kept him busy, but not too busy to cause trouble in Ballymurn. The signs of discontent became visible to outsiders when a row broke out involving the local national school and ended in a boycott by parents. The school lay empty as parents kept their children away in protest at the choice of a new full-time teacher. The favoured choice of parents and parishioners was a substitute teacher who had been working in the school since September, Gerry Normoyle.

At the centre of the row was a decision in November 1991 by Fortune, who was chairman of the school's board of management, to ask the chairman of the parents' council for his views on the appointment prior to the holding of interviews. As a result of his conversation with the priest, the chairman subsequently held a meeting with parents and sent a letter to Fr Fortune about Mr Normoyle, which the parents of children in the teacher's class signed. In it he was described as an excellent teacher who had brought a huge improvement in his pupils during his short time in the school. It seems that by doing this they played into Fr Fortune's hands. He presented the reference to others on the school's board of management as an attempt by the parents to influence the selection procedure and another candidate was chosen.

The parents decided on a boycott because of the failure of the board of management to explain their decision. At a village meeting it was decided to withdraw all financial support to the school and the church. The parents' council wanted the appointment rescinded and a new set of interviews held. Council members met with Dr Comiskey, explaining their reasons for the boycott.

A Message from Heaven

In the middle of the boycott, Avril Doyle, local Fine Gael senator and now also an MEP, decided to pay a visit to the school in an effort to see if any solution could be found. When she arrived at the empty building, she went to look for the three remaining teachers and located them in a classroom where Fortune was talking to them. She attempted to go inside but Fortune put his foot on the door, and through a glass panel she could see him wagging his finger at her, indicating that he was not going to allow her access. She had no choice but to leave.

After discussions with the interested parties, the Department of Education announced that proper procedures had been followed and that it would be approving the disputed appointment. The parents were unhappy for a number of reasons, but they had guaranteed Bishop Comiskey that they would abide by the decision of the department. Three weeks after it began, the boycott ended with parents passing a vote of no confidence in the board of management. At the end of it all, Fortune had added many more to the list of people who did not like him.

As the discontent grew it was noticeable that an increasing number of people had begun to by-pass Ballymurn church and to go to mass elsewhere. Fortune seemed undeterred, although probably upset at the fall in parish dues.

Fortune's supporters were delighted when he put forward the idea of community employment schemes for the area. Given his record in Poulfur, he was clever enough to stay out of the picture when the application was being made for the scheme by the Ballymurn Development Association. Old patterns were soon being repeated, however. Fortune began docking money from the scheme workers, telling them it was for administrative fees. In fact, according to a FÁS source, the full amount was being paid directly to the workers, but they were then "voluntarily" handing over money to Fortune, up to £6 a week for an ordinary worker and £19 for a supervisor.

In frustration local people decided to contact Bishop Comiskey about the schemes and ask him to do something. A parishioner wrote in June 1992 expressing concern about Fortune's involvement. He received a prompt but brief reply from the bishop, telling him that he would "certainly look into the matters raised in your letter but I think that the best thing you could do would be to contact FÁS directly".

Two months later, the bishop responded to a letter from another parishioner, since deceased, saying that there had been discussion for some time about Fr Fortune's "dissociating himself from further FÁS schemes due to an increased priestly and media workload".

The letter went on to state: "This is in no way a reflection on Fr Fortune, about whom I have received the highest reports from FÁS offices in Wexford and Waterford. In view of this I haven't the slightest objection to the Ballymurn Development Association's continuing with a FÁS scheme on condition that they no longer call upon the services of Fr Fortune, specifically in the area of FÁS schemes or anything connected with such schemes. After that, it is really a matter for FÁS and the Local Development Association to decide."

The apparent lack of action by the semi-state body seems quite remarkable. However, a spokesman for the organisation said an independent panel vets all applications and that each scheme is subject to ongoing inspection and audited by an external auditor. The Ballymurn schemes had undergone these procedures, and to their knowledge no financial abnormalities were discovered. According to their records, Dr Comiskey did inform them in March 1992 that Fr Fortune would no longer be involved in the FÁS schemes. He was unsure why the bishop found it necessary to write to them on the matter, except perhaps as a matter of courtesy.

Despite what his bishop said, Fortune continued his involvement with the schemes. The divisions in the community became wider, and resentment threatened to boil over. Letters went back and forth between local organisations in pro- and anti-Fortune camps. As splits developed, there were rows over demarcation between two groups involved with FÁS over issues such as who was responsible for clipping, mowing and strimming of the green areas of the village and the upkeep of the GAA grounds and the local cemeteries.

Another local man who says he made a direct complaint to FÁS was told that the priest would not have any more control over administration. However, in Ballymurn it was clear that Fortune was still pulling strings from the sidelines. In April 1993, FÁS responded to a query from Fine Gael Deputy Ivan Yates about the Ballymurn schemes. The Wexford TD had made representations to the then minister for enterprise and employment, Ruairí Quinn, with a complaint from a constituent. The response stated that there was no evidence of misappropriation of funds and that administration was to the highest standards. The projects had already been monitored many times, said FÁS, but in light of the complaint further in-depth monitoring would be done. In conclusion the letter said that FÁS would be giving "very careful consideration" to any further application from the Ballymurn organisations.

"A number of people complained to FÁS. They could have done a lot more, but the difficulty was that Fortune would pull a few tricks, maybe giving money to someone locally to keep quiet. He made it very difficult to pin anything down," explained a local man. "No one knows the exact amount he made but he did very well out of it."

Adding to the financial intrigue surrounding the priest was a report he made to the local gardaí of a robbery in his house which occurred on 1 October 1993. Fortune told them that while he was in Dublin someone had broken into his house and stolen £13,500 cash from the safe. Of that, he said, £10,000 had been a donation from a parishioner to the Church.

Gardaí examined the safe and found that it had been "burst open". They launched an investigation but were unable to find the culprits. Villagers were further shocked when the local credit union was robbed a month later. Two men held up two officials who were locking up for the evening, forcing them back inside, and £5,000 was stolen. That crime also remained unsolved.

A man who knew Fortune through the Pioneer Abstinence Association described the priest's time in the area as "torrid". His own experience was of Fr Fortune's trying to bully his way into getting a silver pioneer pin which is presented to people who have been pioneers for twenty-five years.

"As the curate he would automatically be spiritual director of the Association. He came to a meeting and he said he was a pioneer. Every few years we would have a little 'do' below in the church with mass and a presentation for silver and gold jubilarians. He told us he was twenty-five years a pioneer and he wanted a pin. We didn't know what to do. I discussed it with a nun that I knew, and she laughed herself sick at the thought of it and said there was no way he was going to get one as it would only make a mockery of the Sacred Heart. We never saw him going into a pub, but we knew he drank socially and in his own home.

"If you claim to be a pioneer, the person you are letting down if you drink is yourself. It's a personal thing. Whether you are a pioneer or not, you just don't go telling lies about the Sacred Heart. You wear the emblem, not because you are a goody goody, but because when you go into a pub people will know that you do not want a drink.

"Fr Fortune said he had joined the organisation late but that he had been a pioneer on his own before joining a branch in Dublin. He was told that proof was needed of which branch and he said that branch was now extinct. We spoke to another priest about it and he also said 'no way' and laughed at the notion of it. On the night that the matter was to be decided, we all made sure to turn up. The 'do' in the church was in about three weeks time. He asked the chairwoman about his badge. At this stage we had proof that he wasn't a pioneer and we told him. He hit the table a wallop with the pioneer book. The women jumped. He went berserk. One of the big fellas there said, 'Father, there is no need to get upset or to fool us. You have been dictating to the women and putting fear in them.' He turned to me and said he hadn't seen me at the meetings recently and said it had been a set-up. I told him he was dead right, that I had not been at the meetings and the reason was because he was there. Then he started cursing – fucking and blinding – we got half afraid of him in case he would curse us."

The man also remembers Fortune's involvement with a wealthy woman whose husband had died and who was now sick herself. She would travel miles from her home to mass in Ballymurn. "Fortune knew damn well that she had loads of money and told her that he would cure her. I know that she wrote out a big cheque to him. That all happened shortly before he left. She stopped coming to mass here then. I said to my wife that it was desperate thing. She was the loveliest woman that you ever met."

It seemed there was never a time when the priest was not on the lookout for ways of getting money from people. Bil Keating remembers his talking about it during occasions when Bil was invited to Ballymurn.

"He would get me to open garden fêtes and things like that, proclaiming that I worked for RTÉ and his institute. We would be standing there chatting and he would point at people and say things like, 'They just gave me £500,' or 'They will leave me a plot of land.' He seemed to have the better off ones down there in the palm of his hand. It was sickening. One day when I was there, he told me he had to leave to go to a healing ceremony, and he asked me to help him. I told him I didn't know anything about such ceremonies, but he said it didn't matter, and that when he winked I was to come up and read. It was very odd."

So many of the Fortune episodes are strange, but a particularly odd one was when Fortune turned up at the home of a Ballymurn man and his mother in the company of a visiting priest. The two priests arrived at the local farm demanding to know why the woman of the house had not attended a particular ceremony in the church in Ballymurn. Upset after the incident, which occurred in 1993, her son Peter (not his real name) wrote to Dr Comiskey to complain.

He explained in the letter how the visiting priest had entered their home without knocking, while Fortune remained in his car. He had questioned Peter's mother in a very aggressive manner as to why she had not gone to mass. Peter, concerned for his mother who suffered from high blood pressure, went outside to ask Fortune to intervene. When he received no response, Peter left to ask a member of the parish council who lived near by to make contact with the parish priest. As he was walking away from the house, Fortune followed him. Peter ran to get away from him. Unable then to make contact with the parish priest, he returned home. By that time the two priests were outside in the car. As Peter walked by he could hear Fortune saying, "Here he comes." The other priest jumped out of the car and approached him.

"He waved his fist at me and repeated, 'I'll see you again.' I replied that I did not wish to see either himself or Father Fortune, but he kept speaking to me in an aggressive manner, stating that I was only making it worse for myself," Peter wrote in the letter to the bishop. "On hearing this statement, frankly I got very annoyed, and I told him in no uncertain terms that I would not allow either myself or my mother to be subjected to this kind of harassment and asked that he please leave us alone."

A short time later, Peter received a visit from the gardaí. Fortune had called them, claiming that his car had been blocked deliberately in the laneway. After Peter explained what had occurred they left. "I assumed that this was the end of the matter and did nothing further," continued the letter. However, a few days later the priest involved arrived at the house again.

On that occasion the priest said he came in peace and without the knowledge of Fortune. However, Fortune was parked at the top of their laneway. The priest insisted that he wanted to speak to Peter on his own, since he had "got away" the previous night. Peter refused. The priest told him that he was in an awful lot of trouble and kept insisting that he wanted to speak to him on his own.

"At this stage I became very concerned as to what I considered to be a very sinister threat," said the letter. A friend who was present pointed out to the priest that he was on private property and requested that he leave, but the priest said he was free to call to any house in the area and do as he pleased. Two other friends of Peter's arrived and also told the priest to go. Eventually he left.

"In normal circumstances, one would have no objection to a curate, missionary or any priest calling to one's house, but these visits by Fr Fortune and the other priest were nothing more than harassment of a most sinister kind which will not be tolerated. I would urge you to ask Fr Fortune to cease this activity and not to call to my house or my mother in future. I have previously asked this to be carried out with no apparent results," concluded Peter's letter.

The following week, Dr Comiskey responded to the complaint. He said he wanted to hear Fr Fortune's and the second priest's "defence" of their behaviour. "To do that, I will need your permission to send them a copy of your letter," he told Peter. Later Peter also wrote a letter of complaint to Cardinal Cahal Daly.

He received a brief reply. "I have read your letter and am sorry for the upset you and your mother have felt. I trust that you may both, in spite of everything, have a happy and peaceful Christmas and that God may bless you throughout 1995," wrote Cardinal Daly.

Six months later Dr Comiskey met Peter in relation to the matter. At that meeting the bishop told him, and some others who accompanied him, that there had been a number of complaints about Fortune previously. However, he could not guarantee that he could do anything.

"One man told the bishop that if it was any other parish someone would get up and beat the living daylights out of Fortune. We were shocked when the bishop asked him why he didn't just do that," recalls Peter. "He wanted to bring in the two priests to explain themselves, but we said we didn't want that. We told him that we just wanted rid of him."

After the complaints against him in Fethard, particularly from Paul Molloy, it would appear that Fortune was very careful to leave the young boys of Ballymurn alone. Instead his attentions were focussed on a young man who had moved into an apartment attached to the parochial house. He kept a low profile, and not everyone was aware of his presence there.

The last straw for many in Ballymurn came when two couples in the parish informed Fortune that they did not wish him to officiate at their forthcoming wedding ceremonies. Fortune, angry at the snub, spitefully double-booked the two weddings for the same day and time in the church. Being a small place, it was not long before his ploy was discovered. Such was the anger following this episode that a petition was organised in November 1994. Some people were afraid to sign and others simply did not want to, but in the end some fifty signatures were gathered requesting "a change in the curacy". It was sent to Dr Comiskey. They waited but there was no response.

Less than five months later, in March 1995, Fr Fortune, to the great relief of many, left the parish. "He said mass in a very hurried fashion and he and his 'partner' who was staying in the house were collected by two guys and bundled into a car. It all seemed very rushed," recalls a man who had been in the village that morning and witnessed the hurried departure.

Subsequently a van arrived to collect his belongings from the house. Some time later, prior to the arrival of his replacement, parishioners noticed that there was a foul smell in the house. Upon investigation they discovered that a rat had died under the stairs. During the search for the dead rodent, they came across a number of magazines which had tumbled out from a hiding place there. Disgusted to see that they depicted child pornography and sexual activities involving men, they made a bonfire and burnt them.

After Fortune left Ballymurn, a letter was read out at masses from Dr Comiskey. It paid warm tribute to their former curate. "Fr Fortune, for his own personal reasons, sought to be relieved of his post as curate and will not be returning to Ballymurn; it does not reflect in any way on his standing as a priest." Dr Comiskey said he was aware that the people of Ballymurn would join him in thanking Fr Fortune and expressing appreciation for all the good which he had accomplished. The entire thing was a surprise, but then the parishioners were used to surprises from Fortune. He could never be accused of being boring. What the letter did not state, and what many may not have known at the time, was that allegations of sexual abuse had been made against their curate and that he was under investigation.

The next time the bishop made contact with Ballymurn concerning Fortune was in May 1995. Although he finally responded to the petition that had been sent the previous November, people were left more baffled than ever by the latest communication from Dr Comiskey, which stated:

Control

I write in response to a document handed in here some time ago. The source of my confusion is that the document was marked "Private and Confidential".

The document was in the nature of a petition signed by several people. You must know that any such document cannot be treated as "Private and Confidential" and is recoverable.

The person against whom the accusations are made has the right to see who is making the accusations against him. The star chamber is no longer in operation.

In addition, his legal people have asked for a copy of this and I have given it to them since it is recoverable. It is not beyond the bounds of probability that the Garda Síochána will also wish to recover this document. I let you know this so that you may be able to inform the signatories of this state of affairs.

God's blessings and kind regards.

Chapter 9

Telling the Story

NEW YEAR'S EVE 1994. That night Colm O'Gorman's father told his son that he "simply could not cope with it any more". He was referring to the sexual abuse suffered by his son at the hands of Fr Sean Fortune, which had been the cause of untold pain within their family for a long time. Now he wanted justice for his son. For Colm, his father's words were the spur that he needed. The statement he would give a few weeks later to Detective Garda Pat Mulcahy from Wexford garda station would set in train a number of events, including Fortune's departure from Ballymurn.

At that time Colm lived in London. It had been many years since he had consciously thought of Sean Fortune and what he had been done to him at the house in Poulfur. But the memories had come rushing back the previous September when his sister was invited to the wedding of a relative in Ballymurn. Afterwards she told him that she had been disturbed by the way Fortune had been hanging around young boys.

"It was the first time I had consciously started to think of it in a long time. Initially I thought I might write to the bishop, but then I just spent more time thinking about it. It was when my father spoke about it that New Year's Eve that I knew I had to do something. I made my statement in February. Afterwards the system would fail me in other ways, but I have to say the gardaí were fantastic. Pat Mulcahy was incredible. He never pushed me or demanded. He believed in it and that was very important to me at the time."

Colm made his statement over two days. On the second day, they got into Mulcahy's car and drove, with one of his sisters, to Poulfur. The memories were horrible, but Colm knew it was a necessary part of telling his story. His recollections of exactly where the abuse had taken place were vivid. Afterwards they stopped in a local pub for a much-needed pint.

The relief of finally knowing something was to be done made the process easier for Colm. The previous years had been tough. The abuse he had suffered had resulted in his leaving home as a teenager, with no money, for a precarious life in Dublin. He lost contact with his family and for a long time life was not pleasant. What had happened to Colm had been very difficult for his father to bear. According to his sister, their father suffered hugely during those years when Colm was lost to him. "He didn't sleep for ten years. He felt it was his fault and that he was a bad father."

One afternoon she came across her father sitting in a room crying. Minutes earlier he had been speaking on the telephone to Colm. When she gently inquired what it was that had upset him, he replied, "I just told him I loved him." It was the end of a long and fraught emotional journey between father and son.

Clearly the reconciliation between the pair is something which Colm cherishes. "I did it [made the complaint] for my father, too. He died in December 1995. The day he found out he was dying, he said he wanted to live long enough to see this through. He wanted the truth to come out and for people to face up to what they did. He really wanted that for me. If he had been here . . . he's a constant source of strength really. He would have been fully behind me. He went so far inside himself to get to a place where he could understand where I was coming from and to forgive himself and realise it was not his fault. We had a tough time and were not really speaking to each other for around twelve years. It was very difficult for both of us. But when he went for it, by God, he went for it. When I finally stopped blaming myself for what happened, it really brought us closer."

Not long after he took Colm's statement, Pat Mulcahy became aware that he had one of the biggest cases of clerical abuse ever investigated in the state on his hands. He knew he was dealing with something which could potentially explode in his face. That knowledge made him exceptionally cautious in his approach.

The obvious place to start the investigation was in Poulfur. He made contact with local Garda Sergeant Kevin Quigley who was stationed in nearby Duncannon. The pair were given as much time as they needed for the investigation. It was not long before they went to talk to Sean Cloney, who provided crucial assistance when he handed over scrapbooks which had been carefully filled by himself and his daughter Mary. The scrapbooks detailed Fortune's time in Fethard and, most importantly, included the "Local Notes" written by the priest which described all "his" organisations and the people involved in them. This self-promotion in the local newspaper during that time would prove crucial in tracking down other young boys who might have been abused. The two gardaí wrote down the names of all the young men who were mentioned.

Mulcahy and Quigley spent practically every day, from morning until late at night, for three weeks talking to people in Fethard about Fortune's time there. It was harrowing. The more they dug, the more they got. They began to work meticulously through the list of names made out from the Cloney scrapbooks. In the course of one interview they might be told the name of another boy or boys. They heard the story of the boy who ran away from the priest's house; the boy who had been imprisoned in the house; the boy from Wexford who would be seen there at weekends. They heard of the boys who were now living abroad and rarely came home. The two gardaí sought their addresses and wrote to them. Some wrote back telling of their experiences. They promised to give statements when they next visited home. These letters were added to the rapidly expanding file.

A horrible pattern began to emerge. The stories of the abuse suffered were all sickeningly similar. Sean Fortune had a clear modus operandi. He would question the young boys on intimate matters – their feelings about girls, then their feelings about boys and how they felt about sex – manipulating their answers. Afterwards they would feel compromised. From there he would begin touching and abusing them. They were not easy stories to tell, or to listen to, but for the boys and their families the investigation was the end of a long wait. Most tragically, the two gardaí heard of two suicides by young men in the area and a third which had been attempted. No official link could be made, but the more they heard the more likely it seemed that there might have been a connection to the priest.

The other disturbing aspect to the investigation was the information that the gardaí did not receive. Some parents, who still refused to believe ill of their former curate or simply did not want to get involved, would not allow their children to speak to the two investigating gardaí.

One of the boys no longer living in Fethard was Paul Molloy. It was around seven years since he had made his complaint to the Church when his mother Eileen told him that a garda investigation had begun into allegations of sexual abuse against Fortune. Paul's name had been mentioned as one of he boys who might wish to make a complaint. By then, he says, he was ready to cope with the risk of exposure that a criminal court case would bring.

"The news of the investigation just seemed to open up the floodgates. The gardaí were very serious at the time about investigating the allegations. My name got mentioned along the line. By then I was old enough and secure enough to talk about it."

In his statement Paul told the gardaí of his abuse. He told of a letter he received from Bishop Comiskey, which would subsequently become a matter of public contention, and how, as far as he was concerned, the matter appeared to come to a dead end. His statement was mirrored by the one made by his mother. During their first conversation with her, Mrs Molloy told the gardaí she had only recently destroyed the letter from the bishop while clearing out the attic. Even at that time, she realised the significance of this and became upset. Later a statement which also backed up Paul's account was taken from Fr Sean Devereux, Fortune's replacement in the curacy.

The two gardaí also discovered that the father of another young boy who had been abused had made a complaint to the Church. In 1990, when Fr Joe McGrath was curate in Poulfur, the man approached him and told him of his son's abuse. The result of this, some time later, was that the man was given the address of a rape crisis centre where he was told his son could attend for counselling. "Fr McGrath told me that he had passed it on to the bishop's office, but they never came back to me to check it out or find out if it was true or anything," the man recalled later.

In Wexford, when Don's father Michael became aware of the investigation, he gave information to the gardaí of Don's abuse and his efforts to report it to the Church. He spoke to Don, saying it was his decision if he wished to become involved in the investigation. He did. In the intervening years, Don had continued to see Fortune around Wexford and he had always feared that the abuse was continuing. One of the last occasions had been a function which was attended by a number of priests and Bishop Comiskey.

"John [Fortune] was there and I met another old Scout leader from St Peter's that I had gotten on well with. I remember the bishop was standing beside me, and John was walking down the steps, and I was looking at him wondering if he would try to talk to me. But he looked at me and then he looked at Brendan and he decided against it. None of the priests wanted anything to do with him that night but he was doing his usual PR job."

The first time that Don ever went into the detail of what occurred when Fortune had taken him to Poulfur and abused him was when Pat Mulcahy took his statement. "I do find it difficult to talk about it. I was very nervous."

Over the years Fortune had kept cropping up in Don's life, either in person, on television or in the newspapers. One night he was sitting at home with his partner Clare watching "The Late Late Toy Show" when Fortune suddenly appeared. "There he was in the audience, guffawing and waving. Clare tried to call RTÉ to complain, but she couldn't get through, and then we noticed that he wasn't on camera any more. I heard afterwards that the switchboard was jammed with complaints. Another night I remember I was in a pub in Dublin and I saw him coming on this RTÉ religious programme. I was with friends, and I told them that I had been queered up by him and they all started jeering at the television. At one stage I wrote a twenty-page diatribe to the bishop asking why he left him keep on his collar, why he hadn't done something. Of course I didn't send it."

Bishop Comiskey was informed of the investigation. About a month into it, he supplied gardaí with the name of a young man from outside County Wexford who had made contact with him in 1986 regarding Fortune. Two years prior to that contact, the young man had been in Fethard on a retreat at the invitation of the priest. The group were members of a youth group, and on the day of their arrival they had been discussing problems associated with that group when Fortune turned up to say hello. They told him of their difficulties, and with his usual disrespect for the truth, he said he was the best person to help them because he had held "important positions" at Maynooth where he had dealt with this sort of thing all the time.

Afterwards he told the small group that he would gladly spend some time chatting to anyone with a personal problem. Questioning young men on this kind of topic was a favourite pastime of Fortune's, but the young man in question, who at that time was indeed unsure of his sexuality, was not to know this. When the priest put it to him that he thought he suffered from a "sexual problem", he confided that it was true. Fortune responded by telling him that he had been spiritual director to a gay group in Maynooth and could help him. Afterwards he singled out the young man and, saying that they needed to talk more, invited him back to his house to stay the night. Once they arrived there Fortune manoeuvered it so that the pair of them ended up in bed together. The priest immediately began to make advances which culminated in his buggering the young man. When he became upset, the priest told him not to worry, that although he may not have realised, it was what he had wanted all the time and that with time it would get better. He then told him to go into the spare bedroom because his housekeeper would be arriving shortly and it would not look good if she saw them both in bed together.

The young man suffered a lot of distress after the incident and eventually confided in a friend, who made contact with Bishop Comiskey. The bishop met with the young man in his home town in December 1986. Dr Comiskey, he said, asked him to go into the detail of the abuse and took notes during the meeting, which lasted for about an hour. Afterwards he told him that Fr Fortune had been relieved of his duties and was convalescing at a retreat house somewhere in the country. The unhappy young man said he was thinking about going to England. Dr Comiskey, he said, told him this was not a bad idea as he obviously needed a break. Two weeks later he emigrated.

Initially the gardaí had difficulty chasing down the young man because the name given by the bishop, while similar to his surname, was not the correct name. Eventually, after months of effort, Detective Garda Pat Mulcahy traced him and included his statement in the file. His story of being brought to Fortune's house, how upset he was afterwards and the meeting with the bishop was corroborated by statements given by others who had been on the retreat. A friend who had gone with him to meet the bishop, but who had been asked to wait outside during the meeting, was also interviewed. Sadly for the young man, his case was later excluded by the director of public prosecutions, who ruled that he had been over the age of consent when the incident occurred.

Attempting to investigate what went on in St Peter's College while Fortune was a seminarian there in the 1970s, the gardaí began contacting other seminarians who had been there at the time. Fr Joe Cuddy, then a priest in Canada, told them he had been involved in the Scouts group in St Peter's. Two young boys had told him they had been abused by Fortune and he said he had mentioned the incident to the then dean of discipline, Fr Paddy O'Brien, and the Scouts Association of Ireland. Fr Cuddy died prior to the case's coming to trial and gardaí were unable to locate the two boys who had made the complaint.

Asked by this author if he had received such a report from the seminarian in the 1970s, Fr O'Brien, now a parish priest in Kilanerin near Gorey, County Wexford, said he had not. "This has been said to me before. I have no memory of it." Asked why Fortune was ordained despite the evidence apparently available to his superiors pointing towards his unsuitability for the priesthood, Fr O'Brien replied, "Obviously he would not have been ordained if we thought he should not have been." He added, after a moment, "He was very industrious."

At that time, in the 1970s, Joe Lawlor was national

commissioner of what was then known as the Catholic Scouts of Ireland (CSI). He does remember a complaint. He had met Fortune on occasion and remembers when Joe Cuddy got in contact with headquarters to report the allegations that Fortune was abusing young Scouts.

"It eventually came to my knowledge from local people that something untoward was happening. The person I would have dealt with was Joe Cuddy. I can't remember was he a priest or seminarian then. At that time he was commissioner for the local groups in the region. It obviously came through to him that this had happened. I never met Fortune on the subject, but I remember authorising Joe Cuddy to go ahead with some sort of inquiry to satisfy himself that there were questions to be answered. As far as I remember, there were a few complaints from local young people. I do remember having to make a decision about what I was told. My recollection is vague, but I think what was being complained of happened over a period and there were a number of different people involved. We would have consulted with Joe Cuddy at the time. The next move was to ensure that Fortune was removed from Scouting. That was the way things happened at that time. Once that was done, I am not sure if there would have been reports made locally to superiors in St Peter's. My determination was to make sure he had no more to do with Scouting, and quite frankly that was the end of it for the CSI. I think he may have made overtures when he went to the North, or maybe it was when he was in Fethard, to start Scouting again. Because of whatever inquiries were made to us, he did not get the chance. I remember it all as being very odd. People were aware of what he was like and it was not normal for people to think like that about a priest in those days. A priest who wanted to start up like that would have automatically got the go ahead," explains Lawlor.

As they came to the end of the investigation, the investigating gardaí sought to interview Dr Comiskey to question him on a number of points, particularly on the cases that they were told had been brought to the bishop's attention. They sought the name of the priest who had interviewed Paul Molloy in All Hallows in 1988 and the written statement Paul had made at that time. A number of efforts were made to contact him by the investigating gardaí. On the third day, the bishop took the call and pointed out that he had already spoken to more senior gardaí and he would not be making a statement. Inquiries by gardaí in Ballymurn concerning possible sexual abuse yielded nothing.

News of the investigation had broken in the media. The first to pick up the story about the investigation into abuse in Fethard-on-Sea was the security correspondent of *The Irish Times,* Jim Cusack. At the time Colm O'Gorman's complaint was made, the reporter had already been making inquiries about Fortune. After the initial report appeared in the newspaper, a youth contacted the journalist and said he had been brought to Fethard in the 1980s by a priest from Maynooth and abused during a weekend stay in the parochial house there.

Meanwhile Fortune was on "administrative leave". After leaving Ballymurn he had moved to Wexford and rented a large house. He told people he was now "staying at Avril Doyle's place", even though the Doyle family had previously sold the house. His prominence meant the case got even more attention than would have been usual. While not initially named, he was described in reports as a "high-profile curate" from Wexford. A number of newspapers published details of his time in Fethard. *The Star* revealed that it had tried to "doorstep" the priest at a "luxury house" that he was renting, but his housekeeper told the tabloid he was in bed suffering from gallstones. A trip he made abroad which included a stop in Brussels caused a plethora of articles speculating that he might be gone for good. Gardaí, on the other hand, were not concerned, because throughout the legal process Fortune had always co-operated fully and they had been assured he would be available for questioning when necessary. It did come to the attention of gardaí that he had transferred £30,000 from a bank account in Ireland to an account for "African missionaries" which he had opened in Belgium. However, the transaction did not become part of the investigation because it did not break any law.

On the last day of March 1995, Fortune arrived, on request, at Wexford garda station, accompanied by his Dublin solicitor, Garrett Sheehan. The gardaí began to question him about the individual allegations made by the boys who had given statements. Fortune's most frequent responses to the questions asked about the various episodes of abuse were "never", "no", "certainly not" and "I have no recollection of that". At the end, one of the gardaí put it to him that there were several allegations of a similar nature.

"Is there any truth in any of them?" he asked the priest.

"None," said Fortune.

"Are they all lies?"

"Yes, they are."

"Why would so many people make up these allegations?"

"I don't know."

He was released without charge and afterwards the carefully prepared file, containing the statements of nine boys, was sent to the director of public prosecutions.

Chapter 10

The Letter

TEN THOUSAND PEOPLE lined the streets of Wexford on the day that Brendan Comiskey arrived as bishop in the Diocese of Ferns. It was April 1984. He had a reputation as a bishop who was energetic, articulate, forward-thinking and media friendly. He was a breath of fresh air and people were thrilled with the appointment.

His own delight was perhaps more measured than theirs. During a press conference, he made a telling remark about how he was not familiar with the Diocese of Ferns. "I feel a bit like Pope John Paul – like a man from a far country." He had come from the state's biggest diocese in Dublin, where he had mixed with powerful and interesting people, to the small see in the south-east.

Nevertheless he began to settle in. According to Ger Walsh, who has observed him as a reporter since he was appointed, he was a bishop who "had the ability to rub shoulders with anyone – from the Bene Merenti medal recipient in a rural half parish to the president or taoiseach".

His sociable nature was apparent from the beginning. Each October he would welcome the Wexford Opera Festival's star personalities to his home in Summerhill for a reception. As time went on, it was noticed that he seemed happier in the company of younger priests, and it came to be said that the older clergy in the diocese were beginning to feel isolated, ignored in favour of their younger colleagues.

A Message from Heaven

Brendan Comiskey was the youngest son of ten children born to a poor farming family near the south Armagh border in County Monaghan in August 1935. His early career in the priesthood was unusual and full of variety. He joined a small American order, the Sacred Heart Congregation, and went on to study at its seminary in New Hampshire and in Rome. After ordination, he went back to teach at a Catholic High School in California. He also taught in New Hampshire and Washington. He loved the openness of the American life, the straight talking and the "can-do" philosophy. He took out American citizenship, maintains friendships with a number of people there still and travels to the US regularly.

At thirty-six he returned to Ireland to be provincial superior of his order. At forty he was secretary general of the Conference of Major Religious Superiors, a post which he made a notable success of. At forty-four he was an auxiliary Bishop of Dublin and in 1984, at forty-eight, when appointed Bishop of Ferns, he became the youngest member of the hierarchy. Great things, it appeared, were in store for him.

But the early promise, in many respects, failed to materialise. The bishop was perceived as being frustrated at being left to languish in Ferns with no bigger opportunity within the Irish Church being presented to him. He was felt to be ill at ease with his fellow bishops. And far from being a native of his diocese, as many Irish bishops are, he knew few people in Wexford. His worldly style and penchant for dinner parties made many suspicious. According to a profile of the bishop in *The Irish Times* in February 1996, he "combined doctrinal orthodoxy with a liberal, worldly lifestyle". Twice Brendan Comiskey was passed over for Dublin and twice for Armagh. He was to rise no further up the episcopal ladder, remaining in Ferns, the compact diocese which included all of Wexford and a small portion of Wicklow.

However, his media profile continued to flourish at a local and national level, and this may have compensated for any possible dissatisfaction with his diocese. There was certainly a strong feeling in the media that whatever shortcomings Dr Comiskey may have had, he was a voice of tolerance and common sense, who was happy to stand up and be counted in a Church where those traits often seemed in short supply. It was to him that Bishop Eamonn Casey turned in his time of trouble. But privately he was an unhappy and brooding man.

As his unhappiness grew, according to observers, it seemed as if his control over the diocese and his priests became lax. More people began to notice his drinking. One priest spoke from the altar about it. It was said that his inebriation was visible on the altar on a few occasions. As his problem worsened, he began to miss engagements. At one time he missed so many that his secretary, who was charged with telling organisers if he was unable to appear, was dubbed the "canceller of the diocese".

There can be no doubt but that Sean Fortune added significantly to Bishop Comiskey's woes, almost from the moment of his arrival in Ferns. A Wexford politician who contacted the bishop on a number of occasions over the years to pass on complaints about Fortune which had been received from constituents says Dr Comiskey's response would invariably be that he had "tried everything" when it came to the priest.

"Every time the bishop had Fortune in to put a complaint to him that someone had made, his response was, 'Where's the evidence? Send it on to my lawyer.' Bishop Comiskey knew there were plenty of allegations, but he got legal advice and there was nothing that he could do when he had no proof."

A priest familiar with the Diocese of Ferns tells a similar story. Fortune, when confronted with complaints that had been made, would insist that he had done nothing wrong, producing documentation or references from other people to back up his side of the story. The bishop was in a very tricky situation, explains the priest, because under canon law Fortune could appeal any attempt to remove him from a parish and remain there while the appeal was being heard by Rome. The priest, quite obviously speaking with the benefit of hindsight, says now that he feels that the bishop should have gotten Fortune into some sort of formal legal proceedings so that he could not, as the priest puts it, "simply bounce in the door and deny everything".

"He should have gotten someone that Fortune was a little afraid of. That person could have held an inquiry. Bishop Comiskey did not ignore the complaints about Fortune but equally he did not do enough. However, I don't know if any other bishop would have done any better. Take one example. He called him in one day and asked him about the money owed to the man in Fethard-on-Sea, which he had borrowed for the telephone system. Fortune had a briefcase with him and he was able to produce a document saying that he had been legally entitled to take the phones with him. What could you do? With a tricky situation like this, the only way to deal with it is to establish some sort of procedure or a tribunal, but the bishop did not do that. I think he would have acted much more quickly if there had been a way around it. When the bishop would challenge Fortune about his bank accounts he would say, 'I'll show you the statements.'"

Concerning the allegations of child abuse, the priest says that in the beginning there was no gossip or rumours, and when it did begin to surface, "We wondered was it that fellas in nearby parishes were jealous of him. From outside, it looked like he was doing very good work, but as we now know what was being presented to the outside was not at all the reality."

He says that around the time Fortune moved out of Poulfur there was some talk about child abuse, but it was vague and there were no details. "The story I heard was that he was sent for assessment and treatment but got a clear bill of health. The bishop did do his best. He is a good person, really, but not necessarily a good bishop, or a good administrator. He did take the situation with Fortune seriously."

A Wexford man who knows the bishop says he was simply unable to cope with the priest's behaviour. Fortune's uncanny knack for identifying the weaknesses of others and playing on them had also been turned on the bishop. "He told me he dreaded the invitations to Ballymurn. Fortune would always arrange the function for around 11am and then insist that the bishop stay for lunch, where he would dole out the red wine to him."

When the Fortune investigation got underway in March 1995, questions began to be asked publicly about the bishop's role. In the *Sunday Independent*, Veronica Guerin wrote what was to be the first of many articles on Dr Comiskey, Fr Fortune and the Diocese of Ferns. Her article stated that a Garda investigation into allegations of sexual abuse by a Wexford-based priest had begun and that seven years earlier in 1988, the Bishop of Ferns Brendan Comiskey had sent a letter of apology to an alleged victim (Paul Molloy from Fethard, who was not named by the newspaper). A Church inquiry into Paul's allegations of abuse had been held in Maynooth, stated the article.

Dr Comiskey responded by giving an interview on South East Radio in Wexford to discuss his handling of the case. He said he had written no such letter apologising for the sexual crimes of the priest in question. Those making claims about its existence should produce it, he said.

"Normally in such circumstances I would think it quite wrong to make any comment until the law has run its full course. In fact that's procedure; a person is innocent until proven guilty. However, I myself have been implicated in the media in a manner which implies I have acknowledged the guilt of the accused, which would be very, very serious, which I haven't. The national and two of the local media have reported that I have written a letter to the alleged victim and his family apologising for sexual crimes of the priest in question. I have written no such letter apologising for the sexual misconduct of the priest, and I ask therefore in all charity and justice in my own and in the interest of the public that those in the media and those anonymous sources in the Garda Síochána who are quoted and who have made claims about the existence of such a letter simply to come forth with the letter to substantiate their allegations, and if there is any kind of letter in existence purporting to be from me, let us all see it."

Dr Comiskey was asked how the allegations against the priest were handled. On one hand, he seemed to seek refuge in the fact that sexual abuse was handled so differently in the 1980s, while on the other declaring that "exhaustive procedures" had been undergone with regard to the priest.

"If someone came to the priest in the eighties and said, 'Well, in confidence and I don't want to go any further . . .' We can't apply the procedures that we have today to things that happened . . . so, yes, there were exhaustive procedures and assessments over a two-year period in place, and the man himself agreed to undergo these, and I can't speak about the nature of them. They were quite exhaustive, quite responsible, involving highly professional people on this side of the Irish Sea and, as well, on the other side.

"When the record is released after the legal process has run its course, people, fair-minded people, will think, "Well, the Church has done what it could.' Now if I was handling it today it would be quite different."

In an interview on RTÉ Radio 1 he said he wanted "to deny categorically the media report that I simply moved the priest from one pastoral assignment to another". Asked to explain what precisely he had done when he heard of the allegations, he said he had been instructed by legal advisers that he should say nothing about that, at that time. "I will have no problem whatsoever when the case has run its course in letting the public know, and the media know, the documentation, and what exactly I did." Asked about the claim that there was a Church inquiry held at Maynooth into the allegations of one young boy against the priest, Dr Comiskey replied, "There was no such inquiry at Maynooth at any time."

On the offensive, the bishop wrote in a column in the *Irish Catholic* on the "truly sad decline in standards of journalism". Again tackling the issue of the letter, he said that the then garda superintendent in Wexford, Superintendent Noel Smith, had categorically denied the claim that the investigation had established that a letter had been sent.

> In last Sunday's *Independent* Ms Guerin now quotes her sources as telling her: there was no mention of sexual abuse in the letter at all. But that was precisely the substance of Ms Guerin's remarks and other media's remarks throughout the past week. Ms Guerin still claims there is now some other type of letter from me, and so I asked for the letter to be published. After all, neither she nor anyone else has claimed that the letter has been destroyed. If Ms Guerin claims to have seen it, what is preventing her from getting a copy of it? Let us all see it.

He went on to say that no clerical board had been appointed by the hierarchy; the alleged victim was never brought to Maynooth for interview; nor did the priest to whom he reported the matter ever visit Maynooth for that purpose.

In fact the Guerin article on the second Sunday quoted Paul Molloy as confirming he had indeed received a letter from the bishop and his memory of what the letter had said.

However, Bishop Comiskey was engaging in semantics. He was correct in saying that it was not an explicit letter of apology. Today Paul says he cannot remember the exact wording of the letter sent. What he does remember is the tone of the letter. He remembers that the bishop spoke about things like "your time of trouble" and "sorry about the matter at hand", with no direct reference to sexual abuse. Bishop Comiskey was quite correct when he said that a Church inquiry into Paul Molloy's abuse did not take place in Maynooth. It had in fact taken place in All Hallows in Drumcondra in Dublin. This was where Fr Sean Devereux had brought Paul in 1988. Unfamiliar with Dublin, Paul was confused about the location and had remembered it as being Maynooth. However, he was certainly not confused about what had gone on that day and had a very good recollection of events.

As Eileen Molloy has explained, she had no reason to lie about the letter. "Of course he sent a letter to my son. I cannot believe or understand why he would say he didn't. I read it myself. It's not every day or just anybody who gets a letter from the bishop. Why would I say he sent a letter if he didn't? We have nothing to gain from it. I don't want to cause trouble for the bishop, but I cannot understand this. I told the truth to the gardaí."

It is nothing new for an Irish bishop to take the media to task over a specific issue. However, the exchanges between the *Wexford People* and Dr Comiskey – a bishop and his local newspaper – during this period, while the Fortune case was being reported, were unprecedented. Editor Ger Walsh wrote each week about the controversy. "It could have destroyed my career at the time," says Walsh, now managing director of People Newspapers, "but it didn't."

Responding to the criticism about falling journalistic standards, the newspaper said that what the bishop had failed to grasp was that it was only the very highest standards in most sections of the Irish media which had kept some of his more unfortunate moments over the years off the front pages. In its defence, Walsh wrote a hard-hitting article, on 30 March 1995, stating that the newspaper, in its reporting, had merely carried the "different claims which had been carried by various sections of the media and on the part-Diocesan-owned South East Radio over the previous weekend and again early last week". He pointed out that before doing this, he had set about getting an official view from the diocese.

Once he became aware that Dr Comiskey had returned from a trip to the US, he immediately left a message on his answering machine.

On telephoning the Bishop's residence shortly before 10am on Wednesday to enquire whether or not the bishop had received the message, we were told by the secretary that she was not aware of any messages. The answering machine had been unplugged before she arrived for work. However, there was an assurance that all messages left would have been forwarded. It was indicated that it was not possible to speak to the Bishop at that point because he was on his way to a confirmation ceremony in Newbawn. Neither was it possible to contact him in Newbawn because he would go directly to the Church and not the priest's residence. However, within a matter of a few minutes the Bishop's office telephoned back and Dr Comiskey was put through. Following a brief "off the record" conversation with the Bishop he read the short formal statement which he was issuing to the media. When that conversation had concluded we were left with the clear impression that some sort of letter had been written by the Bishop in relation to matters connected with the priest currently under investigation.

It was understood that because of legal constraints the Bishop could say no more until the Garda investigation reached its conclusion. It was, therefore, with some disbelief that we learned of the Bishop's statement of denial [concerning the letter] just over a day later. The Bishop's statement of Thursday night/Friday morning was a total reversal of his position on Wednesday morning. He now seemingly had no legal advice bar saying that he never wrote a letter of apology to the victim of the alleged abuse. He also used the statement to attack a number of named publications including this newspaper. He had absolutely no reason to attack us because everything published by us were matters of fact at the time we published them. We made NO allegations. We merely reported on a developing situation within the Diocese and we had given Bishop Comiskey an opportunity to comment in detail on the suggestions in so far as they referred to him. In these circumstances we fully stand over our story of last week. We have nothing to justify or to apologise for. However, we are not surprised by Dr Comiskey's inclusion of this newspaper in his general statement criticising other media. This is not the first occasion on which we have been the innocent victim as Dr Comiskey sought to mow down media messengers by shooting in all directions when he did not agree with something that had been published.

Dr Comiskey, it stated, had more reason than most to know that the newspaper strived to maintain the highest standards of journalism. The article became somewhat cryptic:

To find an example of our high standards we need only recall the circumstances surrounding a major interview he gave this newspaper and *Irish Independent* journalist Justine McCarthy at his residence last May. We are certainly happy that we can stand on our record. Of course the present rumpus has really nothing to do with our standards. Indeed, it has very little to do with the specific allegations being investigated by the Gardaí. But it has everything to do with the perception of how the Diocese is administered, the conduct of certain members of the clergy and the manner in which complaints and problems are handled at top level.

The Letter

The May episode to which the newspaper alluded involved two interviews given on the same day to Walsh and McCarthy at the bishop's home in Summerhill. Shortly after the interview with Walsh started, the bishop produced a bottle of whiskey and invited Walsh to have a drink. As the interview progressed, so too did the bishop's state of inebriation. As the interview reached a conclusion, the photographer arrived and Dr Comiskey said that he had a favourite spot in the garden where he wanted to have his photograph taken. Needing some assistance from Walsh, the bishop led the way to a spot around the side of the house. However, when the three arrived there they found the spot completely overgrown. Another backdrop was found and they returned to the house.

At that point McCarthy, chief features writer with the *Irish Independent*, arrived from Dublin at a pre-arranged time. She knocked on the door and when it was opened she remembers seeing the bishop swaying drunkenly in the hall.

She, Ger Walsh and the bishop sat down for lunch. The bishop got progressively drunker. Walsh had to leave. "I still regret that I left, but I had to go," he recollects. "I had made an appointment with someone else. But of all the people you could leave someone with, you would think that there would not be a problem leaving someone with a bishop."

McCarthy is reluctant to go into detail of what subsequently occurred, except to say that Dr Comiskey made sexually implicit remarks and made "unsavoury remarks about me personally and was threatening in his attitude". On her way out of the bishop's home a member of his staff asked that she would not write about what had occurred. A shocked McCarthy reported the episode to her editor. She was told that a decision had been made that she was not to go into the detail of what happened but to write a more general piece for that Saturday's edition. Over a week after the episode, the bishop rang and apologised to the journalist for his behaviour towards her and the remarks he had made.

As the verbal stones were thrown back and forth between Dr Comiskey and the media during those months, the Fortune investigation was gathering momentum. In June the bishop became embroiled in what was described as the "latest and largest of many" controversies. In an interview with Olivia O'Leary in *The Sunday Tribune*, he called for a debate on the issue of priestly celibacy in the context of the decline of vocations in Ireland. Those remarks brought him into public conflict with Cardinal Cahal Daly, who described celibacy as "the fairest jewel in our priesthood". It emerged at the end of June that Dr Comiskey would be summoned to Rome to discuss his views and his public airing of them.

In mid-July Bishop Comiskey telephoned Ger Walsh, saying he wanted to give him another interview for the *Wexford People*. This time he sharply attacked Cardinal Daly. "This is not a debate about celibacy or indeed the call to have a debate about celibacy. It is about the kind of church we want in Ireland. Do we want an open church where matters can be disclosed, or do we want a closed church where nothing can be debated, no issue raised and where problems are ignored?" He also said that many people in his diocese at that time were far more concerned about Brendan Smyth, the paedophile priest, than about his comments on celibacy.

After giving the interview the bishop left Wexford for a holiday in Kerry. On the day before that week's publication, Walsh was told that the bishop, ringing from a call box in Kerry, was looking for him. Walsh feared that he might have changed his mind about adding further fuel to the celibacy debate, but this was not the case. In fact, the call was to ensure that the piece was being included. The newspaper also carried the results of a survey of priests in the diocese. It revealed widespread support for the bishop, particularly among younger priests, and that support from the public had been flooding into the diocesan offices.

Dr Comiskey spent the rest of the summer waiting for the summons to Rome and trying to avoid the media, which he had once so successfully courted. As the strain became visible, friends were concerned about his health. Photographs of him around this time show him looking gaunt. He made another public pronouncement in late August which many people saw as an exaggerated comparison between the Irish Catholic right and the violently far-right Michigan militia in the US.

Then in September 1995, just over ten years after he had arrived in Ferns, the bishop disappeared. The news broke over the weekend of Saturday, 16 September. The Diocese of Ferns heard from his hard-pressed spokesman, Fr Walter Forde, that he was exhausted because of the summer-long controversy and had gone on sabbatical. The departure was a surprise to all, including priests in the diocese. He had faxed a letter informing all the Irish bishops of his decision on Friday night and Saturday morning. Under canon law, he was obliged to apply for leave for that length of time away from his diocese, and the application had been processed through the papal nuncio.

The plan had been to send a letter to the priests of the diocese on Monday morning and issue a statement to the media the following day. However, Joe Power of the *Irish Independent* got wind of it, and the bishop's departure appeared on the early edition front page of the *Sunday Independent* that Saturday night. Later, the RTÉ "Nine O'Clock News" would lead with the story.

Fr Forde, realising he could not wait until Tuesday, released the media statement. In it Bishop Comiskey said that he had been planning and contemplating the three month sabbatical for some time. "At sixty years of age, after fifteen years as a Bishop, I am grateful for this opportunity for personal growth and development." One of his last acts before he left had been an extensive reshuffle of around twenty-five parish priests and curates. The news of his departure broke over the weekend when many of them were starting in new parishes.

"He is physically and emotionally exhausted. Ten days ago his doctor told him to go to bed and take it very easy, and last Thursday told him to take a complete break. The diabetes which he had suffered from off and on for the last couple of years has also reappeared," explained Fr Forde.

Nationally his sudden departure was linked to a row over celibacy, but locally they were pointing towards the investigation into Fortune. That week the headline in the *Wexford People* stated: "Torment over Child Abuse Adds to Bishop's Woes". The lead story by Ger Walsh stated that the bishop had become "deeply tormented by the allegations and by the fact that he believed the matter was likely to come fully into the public arena before the end of the year". Fr Forde was quoted as saying the case in question was a cause for serious concern, but that it would be wrong to say it was the sole cause of the bishop's current problems. It went on to state that some issues connected with the case "are reported to be potentially explosive from the point of view of the diocese and there is a genuine fear at the highest level over the impact the case might have in the county". Inside it was reported that priests and people in Wexford were largely supportive of the bishop's decision. He would be back in Wexford to celebrate mass on Christmas Eve, it said.

In the absence of the controversial Bishop of Ferns, the media had a field day. Stories about the bishop which had been repeated for years in certain circles were now published. There was frenzied speculation as to what part of the US the bishop had gone and what he was doing. It was left to his spokesman Fr Forde to bear the brunt of this onslaught. As well as continuing with his priestly duties in

Gorey, Fr Forde spent his days trying to answer the persistent media queries, often questions for which he simply did not have answers. Only the bishop had those. On the weekend that the news of the bishop's departure broke, Fr Forde already had almost 100 requests from media organisations all over the world seeking interviews with Dr Comiskey arising from his comments on celibacy. In the following months his telephone would never stop ringing.

On the front page of its next edition, on 27 September, the *Wexford People* again linked the bishop's problems and the Fortune investigation. It stated that the bishop knew that his handling of the allegations of child abuse against one of his curates was "about to plunge him into a serious personal crisis".

"A deeply distressed Dr Comiskey revealed his anxiety when he spoke to this newspaper at the end of August and during a 30 minute exchange the Bishop put forward a proposal which he believed might improve his chances of salvaging his image as the fall-out from the case revealed the full extent of his failure to act," said the article. But the newspaper said that it had had to reject the proposal, and discussion had been abandoned until the exact position in relation to the garda file was investigated.

Ger Walsh says that as he remembers it the Bishop appeared to have just realised that the case would go ahead and that Fortune was going to fight it.

"He wasn't saying to me that he had acted improperly. He was very distressed and wondered if we could get together and discuss us doing a story that would put a good complexion on things. He was worried as to how he would look when all the factors were made known. However, we were speaking about a case which was under investigation at the time and if the newspaper had carried a big interview with the bishop it could have collapsed the case and I was very conscious of that. At the end, as I remember it, he apologised and said he shouldn't have approached me on it."

A Message from Heaven

In the same edition the newspaper told its readers that a request had been made by it on Tuesday, 12 September, the week before the bishop left, for a meeting to further discuss the case.

> The following day the Bishop applied for his sabbatical and by the weekend he was on his way out of the country. The detail of the exchange between this newspaper and the Bishop was not revealed last week so as not to add further to the Bishop's woes. However, repeated denials of our stories linking his departure to stress he was suffering as a result of the child abuse case left us with no option but to produce the evidence to stand up our original claims. The usually confident and upbeat Bishop was in a despondent mood as he struggled to find ways of escaping from a public castigation over his decision to re-appoint the curate to another part of the diocese despite being aware that there were a series of sex abuse allegations against him.

In an inside article, Ger Walsh said that for his part he felt immense sympathy for Brendan Comiskey, the man. "He is obviously a deeply distressed and ill individual whose state of mind is a cause for serious concern . . . The only tragedy for himself is that he did not head out of the Diocese of Ferns years ago. Brendan Comiskey has had a troubled and difficult reign in Ferns with some of his outstanding good qualities countered by weaknesses and poor judgements which left a scar on his own reputation."

The request for an interview with the bishop, he explained, had been passed through Fr Forde, who was not made aware of the subject to be discussed except that it was a matter of urgency "to further discuss matters which had been the subject of a discussion between the Bishop and this journalist two weeks earlier.

"That earlier conversation had been instigated by Dr Comiskey himself and centred on his handling of complaints against the curate in question and how his actions at the time would be perceived in the event of them becoming public knowledge as a result of a prosecution." Six months earlier the bishop had angrily denounced suggestions that he acted in anything other than exemplary fashion in relation to all aspects of the case, said the article.

> The Bishop seemed particularly disturbed by an event which took place in his house at the time. It was attended by himself, the priest against whom the complaints were made and a legal adviser [Fortune's].
>
> It was quite obvious that revelations which were likely to become public about this meeting would stun the public at large and could leave the Bishop looking like an individual who not only failed to pass on the allegations to the proper authorities but who could appear to have considered himself above the civil law at the time. Dr Comiskey went into some details about this event and was extremely agitated about how his actions in relation to it could be perceived in the aftermath of a court hearing. The Bishop did defend his actions but seemed to believe that he would have enormous difficulty in convincing the general public that he had acted correctly at the time. The difficulty for him was rooted in the fact that his actions in relation to this case were totally at variance with all his public statements in relation to child abuse.
>
> It would also be shown that he appointed the priest in question to another parish in his diocese where he would deal with young children again. Dr Comiskey was clearly aware that major questions would be asked about his role in the case and there were clear implications that he had put other innocent young people at risk of being abused.

Recalling his August conversation with Dr Comiskey, Walsh said the bishop at that time had suggested that he might have been better off making a pre-emptive strike. However the editor told the bishop that he could not go along with what he had proposed.

"At this point the Bishop expressed regret for putting me in a somewhat difficult position in relation to the matter," wrote Walsh. "He then revealed that he was to have a meeting with the priest at the centre of the investigation later that evening. As the call from the Bishop was completely unexpected I did not feel I was in a position to proceed on the matter any further at that point. I gave no guarantees in relation to the case and, in fairness, none were asked for."

On that tantalising note, the readers of the *Wexford People* were left to attempt to surmise what had gone on between the bishop and the editor. What Dr Comiskey had actually revealed to Walsh was that he had known about the allegations against Fortune. He told Walsh that he had put the allegations of sexual abuse to Fortune in a meeting at his home in Summerhill around 1987, which would have been around the time when Fortune left Fethard and went to London. The priest's solicitor was present at the meeting. Fortune denied what was alleged and the bishop had believed him.

However, the bishop now no longer believed his priest and he was exceptionally anxious about how his actions would be publicly perceived. What would be said about that meeting at Summerhill? What were the possible repercussions from a trial where he may have to give evidence himself? During the conversation he wanted, according to Walsh, a construction put on the story which would "put him in a good light".

Ger Walsh says that Fortune, who was rambling at that time, went around telling people that if he "went down" he would not go quietly and he would cause all kinds of problems for his bishop. "Fortune was saying, 'If I go down, he's coming down with me,'" Walsh explained. "It is a fact that Fortune called regularly to the bishop's home. On at least one occasion he acted as barman, because I was there and I saw him. The party went on until 4am and as it got later tongues got looser, and there was talk about things in the diocese, including other priests. If that sort of situation was replicated in any regular way, Fortune would have had dynamite material. The day that the bishop made that telephone call to me [at the end of August] may have been the day he found out that the case was going to go ahead or that Fortune was not going to plead guilty."

The week after he left for the US, on RTÉ's "Prime Time", Fr Forde was asked directly by journalist Ursula Halligan whether the bishop had a problem with drink. Clearly uncomfortable, the spokesman said that the bishop had "substantially come to terms" with his difficulty in relation to drink. "In the last year, I suppose he wouldn't have been taking any alcohol for the equivalent of ten, eleven months." Fr Forde denied that the bishop was compromised in any way by a friendship with a priest at the centre of one of the sex abuse cases investigated in the diocese. Subsequently he issued a statement saying that Dr Comiskey had gone to an American clinic for treatment for alcoholism. The coverage continued with speculation on diocesan finances, foreign holidays and the date of the bishop's return.

Although the *Wexford People* received some criticism for its continuing coverage, this was nothing compared to an occasion a few years previously when it had reported another matter relating to the Catholic Church, a 1990 sex abuse case that had resulted in the conviction of a Wexford priest, Fr James Doyle, who pleaded guilty and received a suspended sentence.

In November of that year the newspaper carried a photograph of the priest on its front page and a report of the court case, detailing the conviction. An hour after that edition hit the streets, the newspaper was inundated with calls of protest. That evening copies of the newspaper were burnt outside the main office on North Main Street in Wexford. The complaints continued for weeks. Thousands of pounds worth of advertising revenue was lost in what appeared to be a co-ordinated campaign to hit the newspaper commercially.

Letters complaining about the coverage of the case were sent by the sackful. Around a week later a telephone call was received from a nun in an enclosed order who said that she objected so much she was no longer going to read the free copy delivered to the convent.

Five years later, however, when the newspaper reported, in such detail, the investigation into Fortune and the role of the Bishop of Ferns, there were no ritual burnings and advertising was unaffected.

Chapter 11

A Dual Vocation

IN THE MONTHS that followed, while Dr Comiskey was being treated in the US for alcoholism, it was reported that Fr Fortune had been effectively suspended from clerical duties. Despite the investigation, he continued to turn up at masses, funerals, baptisms and any other religious ceremony, barging his way on to the altar, embarrassing other priests and angering those in attendance.

People could hardly believe it when they saw him visiting patients in hospitals around the county. He continued to offer his services as a healing priest and to demand a substantial fee. Each week he paid regular visits to people in Fethard-on-Sea and Ballymurn. On one occasion his diocesan colleagues were most discomfited when he turned up at a Wexford hotel to participate in a one-day seminar for priests on how to deal with sexual abuse.

In Dr Comiskey's absence, Fr Walter Forde said that there was "no question" of Fr Fortune's ministering at any official church service. However, matters were confused when Monsignor Richard Breen, the vicar general of the diocese, who was in charge in Dr Comiskey's absence, subsequently said this was not the case. "That would be an ecclesiastical judicial sentence by the Bishop on someone who would have merited it and that did not take place. I feel very strongly that it is a gross misrepresentation and is very unjust," he said.

When not making a nuisance of himself in Wexford, Fortune was in Dublin where he was continuing to run media courses, but this lucrative aspect of his life was also coming under scrutiny. A number of articles were published in *Hot Press* in February 1996 about Fr Fortune and his Institute of Journalism and Theatre. In fact, of all the articles published about Fortune and what he was like up close, a piece by reporter Craig Fitzsimons showed just how wacky, bizarre and cunning this man was. When Fitzsimons rang the mobile telephone number given in the *Irish Independent* advertising a "three day weekend media/journalism course, either certificate or diploma", Fortune answered the phone and said that the course cost £300. Asked if he could do any better on the price, the priest knocked £100 off.

Using the name Craig Moore, the journalist went along to the course which was held in the Montrose Hotel in Dublin. Proceedings began with all the students being handed out notes on the subject of ethical standards. These were, according to Fitzsimons, pure drivel.

> The giveaway came when he was actually talking. At first, I thought it was a linguistics lesson. He wrote "Jour-nal-ist" on the blackboard, and explained how the word is derived from the French. Throughout the class, this remained the only thing on the board. "What is a journal-ist?" he inquired, before rhetorically answering his own question. "It's someone who works in the media – or medium – that is the singular of print, television or radio." He went on to explain that creative writing meant "to create something".

Fitzsimons and fellow students were informed that their first assignment would be an essay which would be marked by one of the other lecturers.

"He'll give it a mark," explained Fortune in a painstak-ingly slow manner, "and when he marks it, that should give you some indication of your potential as (pauses and smiles) a print journalist. And the only way you'll learn that (another long pause) is by doing it."

And so it went on. Fitzsimons, aware that Fortune would not be around the next day or on the Sunday morning, absented himself from the course, returning for the final lecture given by Fortune on Sunday evening.

I offered the excuse that my sister had been hospitalised due to an asthma attack. His response was OTT, even for a priest. "Oh, Lord!" he repeated, mantra like, for ages. This gave me the green light to ask him for a quick word. Off we strolled into the courtyard, out of earshot of the class. I inquired as to the exact nature of the certificate.

"What do you mean?" he replied.

"Well, who's the authorising agent? The City and Guilds perhaps?"

"No, it's an independent agency. The Institute of Journalism and Theatre," he answered, like a broken record.

"Well, who recognises it?"

"Well, eh, you see," he spoofed furiously, "ah, 'tis recognised by people who've been given jobs in local newspapers, local radio stations and things like that. Is that a problem for you, Craig?"

"No, not at all. What are your qualifications as a journalism expert?"

"I studied at the University of London."

I referred him back to the question.

"Well, I've none. I'm a priest, you see, it'd be a dual vocation."

"So you're not a member of the NUJ?"

"I'm not, no. No, no, no. I've actually a great respect for the NUJ. They're very good, very good, yes."

This led to a sermon about how he thought the world of journalists and their integrity. I allowed him to babble on for a few minutes (the detail of which you do not want to hear, believe me), but eventually he swung back around to the business at hand. He kindly promised to overlook the small detail that I had missed almost the entire weekend, and said he'd give me a pass, if I did an article for

Tuesday evening. At which point I interjected, "If I'm not mistaken, Father, your diploma results are never below 95 per cent and are frequently 100 per cent."

"That's not true, oh no, that's not true."

"And yet, when they are marked by outside sources, such as the City and Guilds, there are frequent failures. Would you care to explain this incredible discrepancy?"

"Ah, no, that's not true."

"So you deny that your diplomas are useless on the jobs market."

"I do. I do deny that."

It was then that Fr Fortune offered to refund the fee I'd paid, despite a clause signed on the application form stating that the money was not refundable under any circumstances. Sadly, he made the cheque payable to "Craig Moore" – not much use to me. As we parted he mumbled something about how sorry he was for my sister, and how he would pray for her. As I walked away, I reflected that there was something pathetic about his demeanour which, inexplicably, made me feel slightly sorry for him. When it comes down to it, however, the priest has persuaded a significant number of people to part with significant sums of money in return for scraps of paper masquerading as prestigious diplomas and certificates. Considering the amount of money he must have amassed while plying his dubious trade his surname seems curiously apt.

Apparently undaunted by the unflattering piece, Fortune immediately ran another ad in the *Sunday Independent* for more diploma courses. A man named Nigel Cooke came into the picture. He contacted *Hot Press* to tell them his story of having enrolled for an institute course. Cooke had realised fairly quickly that it was all decidedly dodgy.

"To me Sean Fortune is a latterday Chaucerian pardoner, selling certificates and diplomas rather than doubtful indulgences or fake relics. Fr Fortune seems to operate on the old Barnum principle of there being one born every minute," Cooke told *Hot Press.*

Cooke, a one-time local government candidate for the Alliance Party in Derry, had responded to one of the newspaper ads in the summer of 1994. He had been out of work and as a freelance journalist had been unable to find secure employment. "I saw an advert in the *Sunday Independent* about a Post Leaving Certificate Journalism course in Palmerstown Community School," Cooke told journalist Liam Fay. "It was described as a 'third-level course' provided out of EU monies. The exams at the end of the course would, the ad claimed, lead to a City and Guilds certificate. I didn't reckon there would be any problem in my getting in as a mature student because I have a BA from Trinity and I have various other qualifications."

The Palmerstown course, subsidised by the Department of Education and the European Social Fund, had an enrolment fee of £100. Aside from peripheral talks and classes, the timetable consisted of one three-hour lecture every Tuesday, given by Fortune. He lectured there for three years.

> Right from the start I thought he was a chancer. His first lecture consisted of a long ramble about his religious ministry, where he had been, who he had met and so on. He also boasted about the people he had been involved with media-wise. He said he was a media consultant to the Garda Representative Association, and PDFORRA, and he named various other groups. He handed us out homework at the end, requiring us to read his six-page handout which was called How to Write Well. We also had to write a little essay entitled What Makes Me Tick, explaining our motivation.

Handouts were littered with spelling and grammatical errors, and budding journalism students would be offered advice such as "Choose the precious word" and "Use a Saxon word rather than a Roman one". Once, when asked

161

about the number of errors, Fortune, by way of explanation, said that he employed a local handicapped woman to type the handouts for him.

Cooke's second lecture began much the same as the first with Fortune's anecdotes. Then he told the students that he wanted all their home numbers.

Most of the students were 17 or 18-year-olds, just after their Leaving Certificate, and up from the country for the first time. They readily gave Fr Fortune their numbers. They were quite in awe of the man. It was a "yes Father, no Father, three-bags-full-Father" attitude. They allowed him to hector and bully them. But I'd been through college, a marriage break-up, standing for elections on both sides of the border, missing death by inches on Bloody Sunday and various other things. I wasn't going to stand for this. When he came to me I said, "Pardon me for asking, but why do you want my home telephone number?" He replied that he wanted the number in case he had to chase any of us up for homework, slacking, or not turning up for classes. In the previous lecture I had explained to him that I had already been a working journalist, and had done some work for the BBC and UTV and so on. My only motivation was to get the City & Guilds certificate. So I said, "You're unlikely to have any problems with getting my homework in. In any case" – and this was meant as a comic remark – "I've got to this stage of my life without giving out my home number to a clergyman. I don't intend to start now." There was a giggle in the room. But Fortune just said to me, "Leave my class immediately."

Cooke was subsequently suspended by Palmerstown Community School.

They threw me off the course, taking the priest's side. They decided to investigate it without allowing me to have an input into the investigation. I wasn't really bothered because, by that stage, I was pissed off with the course and pissed off with Fortune. I got my money back because, I think, they were afraid I was going to cause a stink. Rather than get into all the legal technicalities with me and argue with an ex-civil servant, they were more than happy to give me my £100 back.

It may have been the end of the course for Cooke, but it was the beginning of some amateur sleuthing into the priest.

I started to do a little bit of digging as a sort of hobby, asking around about Fortune. The name of this Institute of Journalism and Theatre started to come up again and again. One of his handouts in Palmerstown said that the course he was running there was "for" the Institute of Journalism and Theatre. However I couldn't find this Institute anywhere. I enquired from the Department of Education, and other educational bodies. They said that, officially, it doesn't exist. I called on some of my former colleagues in Finance and Revenue and they said there were no tax returns for this body. I checked in the Companies Office, again it didn't seem to exist. It has no VAT number and no limited company status. It has no physical being anywhere. No premises to call its own. As the *Hot Press* article pointed out, it only seems to consist of Fr Fortune, his mobile telephone and his bank account.

Cooke said that in October 1994 he wrote the first of many letters on this subject to Minister for Education Niamh Breathnach. The letters outlined what he had learned about the priest and the Institute. In return he got a series of bland acknowledgements and promises to "look into the matter".

After he read reports of Fortune's being arrested and charged with sexual abuse, he contacted the then Fianna Fáil spokesman on education, Micheál Martin. Martin tabled Dáil questions in November 1995 to Minister Breathnach on the nature of the relationship between

Palmerstown Community School and the Institute of Journalism and Theatre. Martin was contacted a short time later by Fortune, demanding to know what was behind the questions. The response from the minister of education was that there was "no formal link between the Institute of Journalism and Theatre and the programme in the school in question", but added that "some of the materials used on the Institute's courses were used on the Post Leaving Certificate course". She said that Fortune had been selected by the "principal and appointed by the school board of management" and paid "in accordance with normal conditions governing such appointments".

A letter sent to Cooke from the minister stated that she had carried out a thorough investigation of the Palmerstown courses and found "both the course and the quality of teaching to be of an acceptable standard, and the required appointment procedures have been followed". She went on to say that one of the former part-time teachers was now the subject of criminal charges and much media attention. He had been withdrawn from teaching in the school.

Cooke was puzzled by this element of the response, especially in light of a previous *Hot Press* report in which the principal of Palmerstown, Peter Murphy, had said that the "relationship between Fr Fortune and ourselves is an unusual one in terms of employment, so we haven't any records of what dates he was absent from the course".

Cooke could hardly believe it. "This was the main journalism lecturer, absent without records being kept. This is very unusual and a contradiction of what the Minister has stated about how Fortune had been recruited 'in accordance with normal conditions'."

Another school where Fortune worked was Dún Laoghaire Community College in Dublin. The stories from students on the £300 adult-education media class there followed a familiar pattern. They told of the 100 per cent success rate in Fortune's institute exams, where every student would be awarded an A, with a minimum result of 95 per cent and a top mark of 98 per cent. However, there were failures in exam papers certified by the City and Guilds. There were students that liked Fortune, describing him as affable, dynamic and also kind, taking some people on free of charge.

While the garda investigation was underway, Fortune fell back on old tricks and asked people, including his students, to write references in praise of himself. Around this time, in early 1995, he failed to turn up for two weeks running for his Tuesday afternoon slot in Palmerstown and offered students no reason for his absence. Then, at the end of March, coinciding with his being questioned by gardaí, he went missing and, most unusually for him, was not available on his mobile telephone.

"It was amazing the change that came over him. He went from being this brash, ebullient figure, to being comparatively quiet and low key," remembers a former student.

When Fortune returned with six weeks of the course remaining, he told the students that they had completed his module of the curriculum and that he would be personally marking their exam papers. After that he did not return to the journalism course at Palmerstown.

RTÉ distanced itself from Fortune as well, said Cooke, who made inquiries about how the station's name was used on diplomas. "They were adamant that they did not give any permission for the use of the RTÉ titles on adverts, diplomas or certificates." Cooke was told in a letter from RTÉ that the station personnel involved were reminded of its policy in regard to the "identification of a staff member's name in relation to an outside activity being carried out by that staff member".

When contacted for the purposes of this book and asked why he had employed Fortune, Principal Peter Murphy said that he "interviewed him among others. He got the job." Concerning the conditions of his employment, he said, "There are a number of different ways a person can be teaching in a school. He was recruited by the school and selected by myself. He was employed in accordance with the regulations that the Department of Education lay down. The appointment was made to replace a teacher on study leave. The practice in that situation is that while a person is recruited by the school they become an employee of the teacher." Asked about the priest's qualifications for the job, Murphy's reply was that the Department of Education had carried out an assessment of the journalism course. "It was my understanding that he did a one-year course in London and that he was writing for the *Cork Examiner* and involved in South East Radio. By vocational educational standards, he was eminently qualified."

The principal confirmed, when asked, that he had written a reference to Bishop Comiskey for Fortune after the allegations of sexual abuse had been made against the priest. "That's true. I was aware, let's be honest, that there were accusations. I was not aware of whether he was guilty or not, or the quantity of the accusations. He was in the school here, for I think three years, and his basic function was to teach classes to pupils who were, on average, in their twenties. The reference I gave him was basically that there was no sign of misbehaviour here – nothing untoward was ever reported or observed."

He was only in the school for one session a week, said Murphy, and although "somewhat authoritarian, he was pleasant enough. He was in charge and he sort of knew it".

Bil Keating, the President of the Institute of Journalism and Theatre, was also asked to write a reference for the priest. He remembers that between lectures one evening they were sitting in a canteen in UCD. Fortune looked very drained and Bil asked him if he was all right. In response the priest touched his heart and shook his head. "I thought he was ill and said, 'Why don't you take a rest?'

I told him I would look after things provided I had nothing to do with finance. He seemed to think this was a good idea. He gave me a telephone number and told me he was going to see the pope in Rome."

Around two weeks later he returned but was still very down. He told Keating that there was a garda in Wexford who had it in for him. Elaborating slightly, he said that two young men were claiming that an incident had occurred over ten years ago, but that he was perfectly innocent and nothing had happened.

"He explained it in a broken-up sentence. I know it all seems very silly, but for an older person like me...I did not query him. I just said that if he was innocent there was no need to worry about it and he said I was right. Around this time he asked me for a reference for Bishop Comiskey. I didn't care for him at that stage but he was a generous man in some ways. I worked with heroin addicts and he allowed me to give them scholarships to do the course. The gist of my reference was that I had never seen anything untoward happening in the school and he had been very kind to my addicts. I disagreed with a lot of his teaching methods and he was very bumptious. I just wrote simply to say that I found him to be an upright person."

He continued to seek advice from Keating, offering only pieces of the story. His solicitor had said that if he pleaded guilty he would get a lesser sentence than if he pleaded not guilty. "I threw my hands up in horror and said, 'How on earth could you do that if you are not guilty?' He said, 'Oh well, maybe you are right.'"

Matters came to a head in the classroom one evening when Keating found the students handing around a clipping about the sexual abuse investigation from one of the Sunday newspapers.

"There was pandemonium. I decided I had to do something. I told them that first of all I was not the president of the institute and had no shares in it. I said that for all the work I did I got paid £25 a week. I told them that I would do everything I could for them. Someone said that they did not want Fr Fortune's name on the diploma and someone else said they owed him money. Another said they did not believe he actually had an external examiner. Afterwards I talked to him, and he agreed to stay away from the school and not put his name on the certificates. What I did not know was that he was going behind my back and speaking to the students. He had a number of them under his thumb, and they would say the course was marvellous and how marvellous he was."

Fortune was then admitted to St Michael's Hospital in Dún Laoghaire, from where he was in constant touch with the students. Keating went to visit him there. "The story was that he was diagnosed with stomach cancer. I had to go up to see him to get him to sign papers. He did look a bit green, but I think it was gallstones. He had gotten flowers and cards from some of the students. I never said anything to him then about the court case."

His absence from the institute was reported. When contacted by journalists, he assured them he would be returning after he had recovered from his illness. "I absolutely love my work and many of my journalists are working around the world. I will certainly be back, as soon as my doctors allow me and this very day I will be asking their permission. My condition is very serious and I am not out of the woods yet," he said. The Institute of Journalism and Theatre was "completely independent and non-profit making", and in his absence "competent people" were "running the show".

Around this time Fortune telephoned a barrister and told her that he was looking for information on Irish extradition laws to help one of his students who was working on a project. He even offered to pay for the information, but the offer was declined.

Bil Keating stayed with the institute, feeling a loyalty to the students. "I stayed with the course until it ended. The students had a dinner for me, and during it they asked me why I didn't open my own school, which I did. It is very successful. I told Fr Fortune that I did not want to work for him any more, and for a while he employed some of the former students as teachers. He told people that 'the president of the institute is not very well'. I had to write to him and tell him to take my name off the letterhead and that there were to be no other references to me or to RTÉ."

On their last meeting Keating remembers the priest's saying something which disgusted him. Fortune had made a comment that it seemed the case would go on for a while. "He told me it was better that way, that the one thing about being a priest is that you got the best legal advice and it cost you nothing. That made me sick. Afterwards I personally went through hell getting letters and telephone calls from people saying, 'Are you running a school for paedophiles?' They would giggle and put down the telephone. It was quite malicious and totally unnecessary. I was besieged by the press at the time, but I felt strongly that I should be careful about what I said because of the court case. I didn't hate him or anything. I felt sad for him. I don't hold grudges. If something goes wrong I tend to feel it is my own bloody fault, that I walked into it with my eyes wide open. At the time I was very upset. I was still very vulnerable. I don't condone that behaviour or the way that he behaved in the school, or with me, but at the same time I see what was wrong with him as being an illness. I don't bear him ill will. Since then I have got more interested in spirituality and occasionally I say a prayer for him. It was a very sad end. I went through hell, but things have turned around for me now."

Fortune was in Brussels around the time that word came back from the director of public prosecutions to proceed with the case. It was reported at the time that the gardaí had sought a bench warrant for his arrest because he had disappeared and they were unable to trace him. In fact the gardaí had not been anxious about his whereabouts at all. The reason they went to a district justice for an arrest warrant related to the type of charge they had decided to bring. At that point there was some confusion over the date of the buggery charge relating to Colm O'Gorman, so to simplify matters they went on an indecent assault charge relating to one of the other boys. At that time they did not have powers of arrest for indecent assault, hence the need to get an arrest warrant. Once contacted, Fortune agreed to return home.

In early November 1995, over eight months after the investigation had begun, he turned up, by prior arrangement, at Wexford garda station and was taken to court. Dressed in clerical garb, he stood beside his solicitor as Detective Garda Pat Mulcahy told the court that he had been charged with offences on five separate charge sheets, relating to twenty-two sexual abuse charges. He had replied "not guilty" to each of the charges. The state solicitor sought bail of a personal surety of £5,000 and an independent surety of £5,000, which was provided by his brother. He was asked to surrender his passport. Once the case was over, Fortune bowed solemnly to the judge as he left the bench. It was the first of many court appearances he would make.

Meanwhile Bishop Comiskey had been in the US for around six weeks, receiving treatment, and the questions which had arisen on various issues since his departure in September remained unanswered. A pastoral letter read at all masses in the diocese in October said that his departure had not been a sudden decision. It acknowledged that he had a problem with alcohol dependency and had had previous treatment for that problem.

Around this time another case of alleged sexual abuse involving a Wexford priest resurfaced. What would subsequently become known as the "Monageer case" involved Fr Jim Grennan and eleven schoolgirls he was preparing for confirmation in the small village near Enniscorthy.

One afternoon in late April 1988, ten young girls attending the local national school told their principal, Pat Higgins, that the priest had been doing things to them which were wrong during instruction for their confirmation. The episodes took place in the church when he would call them on to the altar one by one, and tell the others to keep their heads down and eyes shut. Once on the altar he would get the girls to kneel and, according to the statements, make them feel his genitals.

The principal – moving very swiftly, given that this was in the late 1980s, prior to the explosion of sexual abuse cases – immediately notified the South-Eastern Health Board. Having received consent from the parents of all but three girls, a social worker arranged for the children to be interviewed by the medical officer of the board's Child Abuse Validation Unit. These interviews took place a week later in the local health centre. The medical officer concluded that the allegations of the girls, aged eleven and twelve, were not malicious, that abuse had taken place and that the children needed protection from further abuse. Gardaí were informed. Dr Comiskey, as bishop, was manager of the school; however at that time he was absent from the diocese. Monsignor Richard Breen, acting in his place, was the person formally notified by the health board through the then director of community care, Dr Paddy Judge. The monsignor told Fr Grennan of the allegations. After Dr Comiskey returned and was made aware of the situation by his vicar general, he apparently suggested to Fr Grennan that he leave the parish for a few weeks. The priest left but would return for the confirmation ceremony of the girls who had made the complaints against him.

Subsequently Dr Comiskey would write to the health board asking for a copy of the report on the matter. It was sent in August 1988, over three months after the allegations were first made.

A Message from Heaven

At that time Jim Reynolds was a sergeant in Ferns garda station in County Wexford. He interviewed the sixth class girls in Monageer in the presence of their parents, along with his colleague Garda Donal Behan. Reynolds says, as he remembers it, that their accounts were convincing and he was confident that the incident had taken place.

"I don't believe children make up stories like that. It did happen," says Reynolds, now retired. "There were other incidents involving that priest. I know that he used to make comments to women on the street. I remember he once made comments to me about a girl in the village who was about twelve. His comments were about her physically and they were quite disgusting."

After the statements had been taken from the seven young girls, Reynolds remembers that he received a telephone call at Ferns garda station from a colleague who told him to immediately send the statements to garda headquarters in Wexford. Normal practice for a garda would be to type up a statement, make a copy as a record, write an accompanying report and then send it on. From headquarters the file would be sent to the director of public prosecutions for a direction on whether to prosecute or not. However, Reynolds was instructed to send what he had immediately. From what he had been told in Monageer and from the specific nature of the statements, he was of the belief that there was enough evidence to prosecute the priest. He waited for a response, but months passed and no direction was subsequently given in the case. He is still puzzled as to what happened once the file left his possession.

"We should have at least have been given a direction to prosecute or not. The disturbing thing for me is that it might be felt that we had not done our job. We did what we were told, but in hindsight we might have done things differently."

Reynolds says it is true that some of the families involved were reluctant to have Fr Grennan charged because of the court ordeal it would involve for their children. However, they did want the priest out of Monageer and kept away from children. When he left the parish as the investigation was taking place, they believed it was a permanent move and could hardly believe it when they saw him return for the confirmation. On the day of the ceremony, the parents of the young girls were shocked to see him on the altar with Dr Comiskey standing beside him.

Jim Gahan's daughter Fiona was one of the girls in that class. "We were given an assurance by the South-Eastern Health Board that he would not be present at the confirmation. Then we saw him walking up the church behind the bishop. There was no way we were going to stay with our daughter, so we walked out of the church." At the time of the allegations against Fr Grennan, there was huge consternation in Monageer with many people refusing to believe they were true. When no action was taken by gardaí or the Church authorities, it reinforced the feeling that the priest was innocent, increasing the antipathy towards those families alleging the abuse. Jim Gahan and his wife Josie had been present when their daughter gave her statement to the gardaí. Knowing that the abuse had been validated by the health board, they and the other parents had waited for a result, but in vain.

"Nothing was done about it afterwards. The truth came out eventually but we had to wait a long time. There was very little you could do against the might of the law and the Church. This community was split over these allegations. It was very difficult. We lost a twelve-year-old daughter in a farm accident afterwards, and we got hate mail saying it served us right attacking the Church."

For their parts, the families involved did their best to protect their children and retreated somewhat confused. An instruction was issued by the INTO, telling teachers in the local school not to allow children alone with the priest.

It was after the death of Fr Grennan that the episode was

revisited, with the revelation that he had apparently continued to abuse until his death – almost six years after the original incident had been reported to the gardaí and Church authorities. The mother of a thirteen-year-old boy from the village, who had served as an altar boy, noticed that he was behaving unusually and seemed disturbed. Then, following the death of the priest, he attempted to commit suicide. The boy was brought by his mother to see a counsellor where he confided that the priest had been abusing him. With the assistance of his counsellor, he wrote to Dr Comiskey to tell him of his experience.

The bishop replied in July 1994. "I am taking very seriously your allegations and ask you to be patient with me while I deal with this matter." He said he would be happy to meet with the boy if he wished. By then, however, the boy had a fear of clergy and did not want to meet with the bishop.

In November 1995, Garry O'Halloran, a member of the South-Eastern Health Board (SEHB), raised the Monageer case at a meeting of the board, seeking an inquiry into it. In a report SEHB chief executive John Cooney explained what action the board had taken in 1988 and its conclusion, following the assessment of the girls, that the allegations were not malicious and abuse had taken place. Two employees of the board had brought the matter to the attention of the gardaí, he said. One of those officers also informed the diocesan authorities, as well as Fr Grennan, who denied the allegations.

Mr Cooney said that the abuse of the girls had ceased following the board's investigation. The children, he said, had come from good homes and had received ongoing support from their families during that time, as well as support from the social workers. Nevertheless the board wished to express its sympathy to everyone involved in the unhappy situation. Anyone who wished to avail of counselling was invited to come forward to the board.

The situation, he continued, had been a difficult challenge for the local officers of the board, especially in light of the very limited resources available to them in 1988 and the generally low levels of awareness of the problem at that time. However, the Department of Health guidelines on child abuse had been fully adhered to in the conducting of the investigation. "We are satisfied that the Board's local staff dealt quickly and competently with the case and not only did they comply with the then recently introduced Department of Health guidelines on child abuse, but they went beyond these," he said.

What is the truth of what happened in Monageer? Even at this remove it is difficult to say with certainty what went on behind the scenes. The village is in the Enniscorthy garda district. At the time Superintendent Vincent Smyth was the man in charge there. Now retired, he insisted when contacted by this author in 1995 that a "thorough and diligent" investigation had taken place in Monageer on foot of the communication from the health board concerning the girls' complaints.

"If anyone was discontented with my action or inaction they should have made contact. There was ample time. I was satisfied with my inaction because I felt there was no scope for criminal prosecution at the time. On recollection I have nothing to fear," he was quoted as saying in *The Irish Times*. He added that he wanted to make it quite clear that Bishop Comiskey had not interfered in any way in the investigation, or made contact with him, as had been previously suggested.

The other garda in the picture at that time was the Wexford-based Chief Superintendent Jim Doyle, also now retired. According to his account, Superintendent Smyth contacted him about the case as soon as he became aware of it but prior to the statements being taken.

"I advised him to go away and investigate the matter. I didn't inquire after that what happened. I assumed there wasn't a case. My job as chief superintendent involved administration, transferring members and advising people on how to do their job. I would not have been involved in something like this."

At no stage, he said during a conversation that took place at his home in Wexford, had he been contacted by Dr Comiskey about the investigation.

Again it was a case of more questions than answers, and the details were emerging as Dr Comiskey was still in the US receiving treatment, so his account of why the priest had been allowed to remain in the parish went unheard, as well as any explanation of any discussion he may have had with senior gardaí about the case. Clearly exasperated with all that was being said about him at home, he telephoned RTÉ radio on New Year's Eve 1995 to give an interview. Monageer was one of the issues he addressed. "To the best of my knowledge, the Garda Síochána have issued a statement since I left saying they could not find cause against that particular priest," he said.

In fact the gardaí issued no such a statement. What the Garda Press Office was saying at that time was that the investigation "stopped suddenly and without explanation", and that it had been the decision of local garda management. A spokesman also revealed that the file on the case had disappeared. What the bishop may have been referring to in his interview was Superintendent Vincent Smyth's explanation as to why the investigation went no further. While his recollection was hazy by that time, Smyth would also say that he had decided not to proceed because the parents of the girls were not anxious to do so, and he was not aware of any gross indecency having occurred.

It seemed at that time as if Wexford had an unusually high number of sex abusing priests, with the case of Fr Jim Grennan being mentioned along with that of Fr Sean Fortune and Fr Donal Collins, the former principal of St Peter's College. Closer to the truth is that the diocese faced similar problems to those encountered elsewhere, except that the cases became well known and questions were mounting about the bishop's handling of them.

The bishop had not returned home from the US for midnight mass in St Aidan's Cathedral, Enniscorthy, as promised, nor on a second proposed date. The next time his flock saw their bishop was at a Saturday evening mass in February 1996, five months after his departure. "Our God has a great sense of humour – I return to you on Temperance Sunday," he quipped from the altar of St Aidan's that evening.

In his sermon he apologised for the suddenness of his departure. He had been unable to come out and state publicly that he was going to seek treatment for alcoholism. He hit out at some of what had been published in his absence. He mentioned his visit to Rome and his meeting with Cardinal Gantin, the Vatican's second most powerful man, who had assured him that he was returning to the diocese with the blessings and prayers of the Holy Father. He stated that his treatment had not cost a penny, contrary to "wild and irresponsible rumours that my stay was costing £8,000 per week or month". He told the congregation that he would, in time, respond to the many other questions raised, but that it would take a little time. The one extremely damaging untruth, he said, had been that he was never going to return to Ferns. He did not mention Fortune by name, but he spoke about the case and how he had been implicated.

> It is a lie to state, as has been done repeatedly, that I "ran away" away from the diocese to escape the pain of confronting child abuse issues. No issue has caused me greater pain, nor has taken up more of my time. Any pain or anguish, however, which I have experienced is miniscule compared with the awful hurt, pain, outrage and anger experienced by parents who have brought a child into being, who have been present at life's greatest

miracle. The wild, sensational and totally unfounded allegations that I would sacrifice the innocence of a child to protect some drinking buddy – or any other buddy – is particularly vicious, untrue and cruel. It would be so easy for me to blame my alcoholism and say it was the demon drink that caused me to make mistakes. The fact is, however, that in dealing with those cases I was never more sober. Child abuse is a very sobering reality. So I refuse to take the easy option of blaming anyone or anything, least of all alcoholism.

I would like to be able to tell you at all times I acted swiftly, prudently and without hesitation when these matters were brought to my attention. Regrettably, I cannot, because in some instances the information which I received was entrusted to me either as a confessor or as confidential under a solemn promise not to be repeated. The conflict of judgement and the crisis of conscience which this created within me compounded my own inner turmoil, the net result of which I made mistakes. Let me repeat without equivocation, I made mistakes. I now stand accused because I now know how these cases – some of which go back to the 1970s – should be handled in 1996. I should have known that fifteen years ago. If that be so, I am guilty. Hindsight is as wise as it is useless. One thing I can say, however, is this, I have never, ever, put a child's safety at risk to protect any priest. I can tell you, most solemnly, that I have always acted in the utmost good faith and have never, ever, obstructed an investigation into the acts or omissions of any priest directly or indirectly under my authority or control. I have never in my life refused to be interviewed by a member of the Garda Síochána. Further, I co-operated fully and diligently with any investigation insofar as I was able to do so. Despite what has been said I have always and will always continue to co-operate with the authorities to ensure that those guilty are brought to trial and most important, those hurt are comforted and healed.

I will continue to pursue these objectives and play a pivotal and forefront role as bishop of this diocese in giving any evidence that I am able to, and provide and furnish any papers or information to the gardaí or the DPP in the prosecution of these unspeakable crimes.

It was a masterful performance. Dr Comiskey was hailed as the hero who had conquered the twin evils of alcoholism and journalism.

"Did you miss me?" he asked the congregation.

"I did," said a woman at the back.

"You should'a said, 'I didn't know you were away,' " he responded, amid laughter.

After overcoming this first obstacle, the bishop now had to answer the reports which had been carried in his absence, everything from the reasons why he had chosen Thailand as a holiday destination to a fuller explanation of how he had handled various allegations of sexual abuse among priests in the diocese.

His friends and advisers had gathered together to discuss the matter. It was decided that on his return he would speak to RTÉ and *The Irish Times* and leave it at that. He took advice from close friends such as John Hynes, An Post chief executive. At that time Dave Curtin was An Post PR manager. Asked by Hynes what strategy he felt the bishop should devise, Curtin advised that a press conference be held and all media organisations be invited to attend.

"I knew that just doing one or two interviews would be like shaking a hornets' nest. I advised on a press conference where he would talk to everyone for as long as they wanted. Look at two past examples and you'll see how the different approaches work. Ben Dunne came back from Florida and by the end of it people got fed up listening to him. Eamonn Casey never spoke to anyone and they are still looking for him."

Noel Smyth, Ben Dunne's solicitor, was also a member of the bishop's inner circle. It had been he who advised

Dunne to bare his soul and express his contrition after he was found with a call-girl in a hotel room in Florida and arrested for possession of cocaine.

The bishop decided on a press conference to be held in Wexford. On the appointed day, journalists from different media organisations arranged to meet in a Wexford hotel to organise, somewhat unusually, to co-operate in order to maximise the limited time available. As it happens, Dr Comiskey handled the press conference magnificently. The efforts by the journalists to put a shape on the proceedings failed quite miserably. He was calm and very much in command of the material he had been collating over the previous ten days. The diocesan finances were dealt with quickly in a flurry of facts. Veronica Guerin was really the only journalist there with the expertise to question him on financial matters, but she became quite flustered when he picked her up on one or two points in her reporting.

"There were a number of journalists and none of them got the chance to get into the nitty gritty of anything. They simply weren't able," recalls Dave Curtin. "Veronica Guerin spent a lot of the time going over the stuff she had written and defending it, and that took up a lot of the time. Of course everyone wanted to get their question in. Bishop Comiskey spent some time preparing for it and on the day he was very good."

The communication skills for which he is famed stood Dr Comiskey in excellent stead as he smoothly fielded the queries. He told the journalists, with their pens at the ready, that over 427,000 words had already been written in the media about him during his five month absence. He issued a "heartfelt apology" to priests and people for his abrupt departure. He had been unable to come straight out and state publicly that he was being treated for alcoholism.

He began by saying that he had "never ever" obstructed any garda, health board or any other investigation into child sexual abuse or sexual misconduct.

I have never ever tried to sweep under the carpet any child sexual abuse allegation.

I have never ever refused to be interviewed by the Garda Síochána.

I have been in communication with the Gardaí in relation to two complaints alleging sexual misconduct – not ten as alleged in one media report.

I have never misused or misappropriated diocesan funds. Not a single penny of diocesan funds or any other funds, such as bequests, under my care is missing. All accounts are in order.

I was never in a Hazelden treatment centre in Florida or any other Hazelden centre.

I never "escaped" or "did a bunk" from any treatment centre in Florida or anywhere else. My treatment in Guest House, Rochester, Minnesota, did not cost £8,000 a month. It cost the diocese not one single penny.

Lurid and sleazy comments have been made about my holidaying in Bangkok. Not a single one of these holidays referred to were in Bangkok.

I have never been arrested in my life. I have never been jailed in my life. I have never been "rescued" from jail by an official of any embassy or anyone else.

I have never been deported from Thailand or any other country.

I have never paid for a first class airline ticket in my whole life.

I always intended to return to the diocese and never ever said I wasn't coming back to a people I have grown to love and among whom I have spent by far the happiest, if challenging, years of my priesthood.

A pretty horrific list of things, all of which I have been accused of, every one of which is simply untrue. Whatever else brought me back, and I was never tempted not to come back, it was worth it all to get that much on the record. But the main reason I came back is because I believe that, like every other bishop, I have, through the ministry of the pope, been given a mandate from Jesus Christ to preach the Gospel in this corner of God's kingdom. I intend to remain faithful to that divine promise.

In one of the sharper moments, he challenged Ger Walsh to produce the evidence that he had denied knowledge of sex abuse allegations against Fr Jim Grennan in Monageer.

He said there had never been a single case of child abuse in the diocese which had been brought to his attention that he had failed to act upon. But a little later he was admitting that his "single greatest mistake" was his "failure to go immediately to those who were hurt and suffering. I went to the lawyers and not to the children and their parents." He had never drunk or gone on holidays with any priest accused of child abuse.

At that time the Fortune case was before the courts and the bishop declined to take questions concerning it. The situation was similar for the Fr Donal Collins case. That left the Monageer case. Dr Comiskey said the "most hurtful" allegations of all those made during his five month absence was that he had obstructed justice in the Monageer case. He said he would go "under oath" before any tribunal to reject this charge. He had worked with the gardaí and the health board during the investigation.

"I did not obstruct justice. I co-operated as completely as I could with the statutory authorities." At the time, he had advised Fr Grennan to see a solicitor and also referred him to a "very eminent" psychiatrist.

The bishop confirmed that he had been aware of the accusations at the time of the confirmation. He had not spoken to any of the girls or their parents at any stage, and he "regretted it absolutely". He had sought legal advice on many occasions about the case and was told by his solicitor to await the outcome of the garda investigation. Under no circumstances, his solicitor advised, was he to get involved "lest it be interpreted as some kind of cover up". The solicitor had told him that he was happy that "everything was being done by the book" and that the statutory bodies were involved in the investigation.

"I have no idea in the wide world, as God is my judge, why that investigation was stopped," he said, adding that it was a mystery. Asked if he felt that he had any responsibility for the fact that no prosecution was brought, the bishop replied, "If the gardaí could not make the evidence stick, I don't know what I could do."

Dr Comiskey said that after the abuse was validated, the SEHB's director of community care, Dr Paddy Judge, now retired, had, in his absence, informed the vicar general of the diocese, Monsignor Breen, that very serious charges had been made against Fr Grennan. He asked that the priest be removed and said he had a programme of treatment for the priest already lined up. Monsignor Breen said he would need to speak with Fr Grennan. Afterwards Fr Grennan had a meeting with Dr Judge, which Dr Comiskey described as "very, very, very stormy and angry". The priest said he had "not been heard". Another vicar general had been informed by the health board, which meant, the bishop said, that at least three senior priests knew before he did of the allegations. On his return from the US, he was informed.

Fr Grennan had always "vehemently denied" the allegations, and the Dublin psychiatrist to whom Bishop Comiskey had sent him said the priest was "completely innocent", a belief shared by most of the senior priests of the diocese. At one point during the press conference, the bishop brushed aside a question as to whether he had accepted the psychiatrist's view over that of the health board, stressing that the key thing to bear in mind was that the gardaí had investigated the allegations against the Monageer priest and had found them insufficient to charge him.

"I know it has been claimed, in an extraordinary litany of things, that I obstructed justice, that I assured the director of community care [Dr Judge] at the time that I would handle the case myself. That there was no need for Garda involvement. And that the director of community care said, 'That's all right but you need to write a letter to the health board.' That I was supposed to have written him a letter. This is all complete fantasy which has, thank God, been verified by both the Garda Síochána and the director of community care." In fact, he added, he had never met Dr Judge at any time in 1988.

The bishop said that, in fact, at the time when the allegations were made it was regarded as enlightened for the Church and the statutory authorities to be working so closely together. He could have laid himself open to a civil action by Fr Grennan.

Dr Comiskey emphasised again and again his total co-operation with the "statutory authorities" and his inability to use Church law to move against Fr Grennan when the gardaí could not move against him in civil law. It was a cogent argument, but there were those who questioned whether it was an adequate response for a bishop. They questioned whether the safety and protection of children had been the paramount consideration when the priest had been allowed back to the parish after just three weeks. Clearly the bishop had been faced with a difficult situation in which there were few easy choices, but some asked was there not more of the lawyer and less of the bishop in his arguments.

Asked if he regretted bringing Fr Grennan, who would once again be accused of sexual abuse, back to the parish, he said there was nothing else he could do at the time. The state, he said, should make it mandatory to report child sex abuse allegations to the gardaí and other statutory authorities.

There was at least one case, an old case, he said, which he did not report to the gardaí, thinking that it would be handled by removing the priest and treating him. Even as late as the previous year, he had "a very vigorous argument" with one priest who said he would never report or inform on another priest. He had removed one priest for an investigation to take place. After "vigorous representation" from that priest's therapist, he had reappointed him after two years, but he would not have done that today. In another case he had removed a priest, but the Human Life Institute in Connecticut, "supposed to be one of the best treatment centres in the world", strongly recommended that this priest "must be given back his post". He had refused and come in for considerable criticism himself.

He had become aware of allegations of child sex abuse against priests "almost immediately" after he arrived in Ferns in 1984. There were complaints already on file. One of those files would have related to Fr James Doyle, who would be convicted in 1990 of the sexual abuse of a young Wexford boy. As it happens, eighteen months before Dr Comiskey's arrival in the diocese, in October 1982, Monsignor E. Feichim O'Doherty, professor of logic and psychology at UCD, had written to the late Bishop Herlihy concerning Fr Doyle. He recommended that the priest should be kept away from young people. Fr Doyle, when interviewed, the monsignor said, "had a clear example of mollities", "which my dictionary says means, in a bad sense, weakness, effeminacy". The priest had a history of "auto-eroticism and both homosexual and heterosexual behaviour" and "did not face up to celibacy in any realistic sense". The monsignor said it was desirable that he should have a change of role, away from working with young people. Around the same time a Wexford parish priest, worried about an alleged incident involving improper behaviour by Fr Doyle, also communicated his concern to Dr Herlihy.

Asked at the press conference if the diocese had any prior information or advice about the risk Fr Doyle might pose to young people and if any priest had warned him about such a risk, Dr Comiskey said there had been "a letter from a counsellor", but his recollection was that it did not mention risk to children. He could not remember any warning from a priest, but asked to be allowed to check his records before giving a definitive answer. Later, a source close to the bishop told Andy Pollak from *The Irish Times*, who had researched the story, that the letter from Monsignor O'Doherty appeared to have been stolen, and in any case it had warned about a different problem, not connected in any way to paedophilia.

The bishop had relieved Doyle of his pastoral duties as a result of the case, and after he received a suspended sentence, the priest went to the UK. In 1994, four years after his conviction, *The Observer* newspaper reported that the priest was now working in south-east London, apparently with the full backing of Church leaders, who had kept his background a secret. People in the parish were angry that he had been entering schools and that they had not been told of the child abuse conviction.

At his press conference Bishop Comiskey did make a very convincing defence of himself. However, the weakest part was his exposition of how he dealt with clerical sexual abuse cases. His responses lacked detail and precision. He did admit that he could have done better, but many questions remained. Concerning the Monageer case, there were differences in recollection between him and former Chief Superintendent Jim Doyle. When questioned initially, Doyle said that once he had been informed of the investigation by Superintendent Vincent Smyth, he "didn't inquire what happened after", simply assuming there was no case to be answered; in any event it was not his job to become involved in the investigation. He said that at no stage had he been contacted by the bishop.

However, at his press conference the bishop said that Doyle had come to him and discussed the case in the last week of May 1988, some weeks after the allegations were made. Dr Comiskey said Doyle had asked him to remove Fr Grennan temporarily from the parish while the allegations were being investigated because emotions were running high. He spoke to the priest who asked if he would be back in time for the confirmation, and Dr Comiskey said he was under the impression the investigation would be completed by then. The priest went to Spain for three weeks with a friend. The bishop said he had not gotten the impression from Doyle that the gardaí were going to question or arrest the priest. However, the chief superintendent had told him they feared Fr Grennan might take his own life and had been keeping a watch on his house.

The night after the press conference, Doyle, when again contacted by this author, pointed out that while he had said that at no stage had he been contacted by the bishop, he [Doyle] had made the contact and made an arrangement to speak to Dr Comiskey about the case. At that meeting he passed on the message from Superintendent Smyth that he had "verbal complaints from parents" about Fr Grennan's abusing their daughters and that they were anxious that the priest "should not appear with the bishop at confirmation". He said it was "not correct from my point of view" for the bishop to say Doyle had asked him to remove the priest or had said that Fr Grennan's house was being watched.

It does seem incredible that after being informed that an investigation into allegations of sexual abuse was being conducted into one of his priests, the bishop was not curious to know the outcome from the gardaí. Did he wonder whether the children in Monageer were now safe or if the allegations against the priest had actually been malicious? What were his feelings when the young Monageer boy contacted him in 1994 to say he had also been abused by Fr Grennan?

If Doyle found the matter important enough to arrange a meeting with the bishop in the first place, it seems surprising that afterwards he himself didn't inquire about what had happened from his superintendent in Enniscorthy.

The Dungarvan councillor, Garry O'Halloran, who first raised the issue with the SEHB, wrote in February 1995 to the garda commissioner and the minister for justice seeking a garda inquiry into the affair. The then commissioner, Patrick Culligan, ordered an inquiry into why Fr Grennan was not prosecuted. He appointed Cork-based Chief Superintendent Dermot Dwyer to investigate.

Almost five months later the Garda Press Office issued a statement concerning Dwyer's report, stating:

> The review shows:
> –that the investigation was inadequate and not brought to a satisfactory conclusion,
> –that the South-Eastern Health Board had complied fully with its obligation,
> –that no evidence was forthcoming of any collusion between any organisation and the Garda Síochána to stifle, obstruct or abandon the investigation, and
> –that no fault lies with the local Gardaí based at Ferns.
> Regretfully as the person who was the subject of the complaint has since died the matter cannot now be put any further.

Asked his opinion of this statement, former Superintendent Smyth said he did not wish to comment. Jim Doyle said that as far as he was concerned the inquiry was finished and he accepted its findings. Former Sergeant Jim Reynolds, who took the statements from the young girls, was pleased that it had shown he and his local colleagues had done their job. The SEHB welcomed the confirmation that it had complied fully with its obligations.

What was not published was that the investigation also found that there had been an unwillingness on the part of senior gardaí in Wexford to confront senior clergymen in the Diocese of Ferns. It said this was perhaps understandable to some given that the case was reported at a time when people were less willing to accept or confront the wrongdoings of the clergy. While it found no evidence of collusion between any organisation and the gardaí, it did criticise Smyth and also Doyle for their reluctance to pursue the investigation in light of the validation of the abuse by the health board. It also pointed out the poor judgement shown in not appointing a female garda to interview the girls rather than local male gardaí, who were known to them, which may have inhibited them in recounting what went on. The girls and their families, it found, had a right to feel that they had been failed by the system. It was easy for Dr Comiskey to say afterwards that when he had not been informed of any developments he had assumed there was no case against Fr Grennan.

Since his bravura performance at the press conference in February 1996, the Bishop of Ferns has maintained a remarkably low profile. The handling of the Monageer case has resulted in a civil action being taken against him, the minister for justice and the attorney-general by Fiona Gahan, now aged twenty-four. Through his mother, the young boy, now almost eighteen years old who also alleges that the priest abused him, has begun similar proceedings.

Chapter 12

"It Was an Awful Time"

THE WAIT SEEMED interminable. The young men who had taken the step of coming forward to the gardaí in early 1995 found themselves at the beginning of 1999 facing another new year with still with no news of a trial date. They wondered if it would ever happen. The weeks of waiting had turned into months and the months into years, the priest using every option at his disposal to try to delay, if not avoid, a trial.

Matters were made worse by his highly visible presence around Wexford where they had to continue to see him. For instance, he called regularly to an old woman living next door to the family of one of the boys, and one evening RTÉ news reported on one of his court appearances in Wexford. According to practice, they did not identify him, but did show his large feet as he walked out of the courtroom. It may have only been this small section of his body, but for anyone one who knew him, Fr Fortune's feet were unmistakeable. The next night Fortune called to the elderly woman, and she told him she had seen his feet on the news. He told her she was mistaken, that they were not his feet, but he would find out whose feet they were and let her know. While most people at that time wanted to run him out of the county, there were those who believed the priest to have been seriously wronged and who continued to welcome him into their homes.

"It was an awful time," said Sean Cloney. "We saw him

going around the place and continuing to call to people and claim that he could heal them. He called to the old people in hospital all the time. He was still trying to get money all over the place. When I was in the [National Rehabilitation] hospital in Dún Laoghaire, he was in the next ward visiting a young fella who had been paralysed in a car crash. Needless to say, his family was very upset. Fortune told his parents in Wexford that he would cure him, but that he needed £50 a visit. He got that and he was also taking money from the lad in the hospital."

The gardaí kept receiving complaints about him, but there was nothing they could do. Fortune was behaving just as he had always done before the charges were brought against him, except that now he was without a parish, his radio slots, newspaper columns and, eventually, journalism courses. He moved into the house in New Ross and named it "Our Lady of Fatima Presbytery". In yet another Fortune-constructed incongruity, he turned it from an ordinary small terraced house into his very own house of prayer. He reportedly held daily and weekly masses, a daily holy hour, healing and counselling sessions. He began ministering to the travelling community. In what was patently yet another fabrication, he told some of his followers that this "church" had been consecrated by Dr Comiskey and that he had not celebrated mass there until the blessing had taken place. He also claimed that the bishop was a regular visitor to the house and that he himself was "summoned" to lunch at the bishop's house in Wexford regularly. Fortune lived in the house for almost three years, but there are no reports whatsoever of the bishop's visiting the priest there. In fact, according to locals, the frequency of Dr Comiskey's visits to New Ross actually diminished with Fortune's arrival there.

During those years he was sometimes seen hanging around the public toilets in towns around the county. At one time gardaí in Arklow, who saw him outside the public toilets there, parked and watched as he made a call on his mobile phone and then got back into his car. They followed him as he drove a short distance outside of the town. He stopped to pick up a young boy who appeared to have been waiting for him. The gardaí moved in. When questioned, the young boy said he had been told by Fortune to give a different name and to say that the priest had been hearing his confession.

As the investigation continued, Fortune turned to Bishop Comiskey for financial assistance, saying that the money from the journalism courses had dried up as a result of the adverse publicity. Given all the money he must have amassed over the years from courses and other scams, it is difficult to imagine him running short. It is clear from the correspondence that the bishop felt the same way.

In a letter to Dr Comiskey's secretary, Fr Tommy Brennan, in March 1996, Fortune said that he had, as requested, furnished an account of his financial situation to Fr Jack McCabe, who was involved in administering diocesan finances. He said he had received a cheque every five weeks for £500 to cover living expenses.

> This has been a great help and it has covered some of my expenses. I have tried to run some media courses but due to the bad publicity I have received, they produce very little profit. The profit from the last media course that I organised amounted to just £47. As I explained to you on the phone, the total profit since last March 95 for the courses was £1000 which I used to pay the Church and General Insurance of £450, £400 to Standard Life Insurance retirement fund and the remainder on car petrol and service. Due to the fact that I had no other income since last March, I had to borrow £10,000 which is long since spent. I have to pay that loan back in due course. I have no other source of income other than the cheque that I was receiving each five weeks from the Diocese. That pays for some part of my expenses which comprise of food, electricity,

phone, clothing, petrol, for and maintenance of the car. I also owe £560 to St Aidan's fund and excess payments to doctors – amounts over the VHI rate. I also owe 48 Diocesan payments. I was expecting the usual cheque on Monday week last March 11th to pay my grocery bills, petrol, ESB, phone, etc, and I can only stress the urgency of this financial assistance until, God willing, I am back in pastoral ministry. I have literally no food in the house and all the bills are mounting up etc, and so I humbly ask for immediate financial assistance.

With many thanks for your kindness and courtesy. I will ring first thing on Thursday morning as arranged. I know that the Bishop is very busy but I asked Theresa a few weeks ago for an appointment to see him. I would be grateful for such an appointment in the near future.

The following month, on Easter Sunday, 7 April, Dr Comiskey wrote a letter to his priest. Fortune must have found it of cold comfort.

Dear Father Sean,

Thank you for your most recent letter seeking financial assistance.

The question of assistance for priests accused of child sexual abuse was discussed at the most recent meeting of the Council of Priests and of the Vicars. It was decided, in principle, that these priests be assisted, where necessary, in the area of maintenance and medical expenses. It was suggested that I explore the whole matter of legal assistance with the diocesan solicitors Kirwan and Kirwan. In addition two priests were asked to study the matter further and to draw up guidelines in an area which is new for us all.

It was also decided unanimously at both meetings that not a single penny from those monies contributed directly by the faithful to the Central Fund, that is, the Envelope Collection, be used for such assistance. Therefore, it would seem that the only real source of revenue would be an annual appeal to the priests of the diocese asking them to contribute voluntarily to this fund.

There is no easy way of putting this, Sean, but the priests are simply unwilling to contribute to you personally for there is widespread perception that you are in employment – offering various courses – and, therefore, have monies of your own. For you to be in receipt of such assistance, therefore, priests would have to be convinced that you are in real need of it, and quite simply they are not at present so convinced. For example, if I were to tell them that you made a profit of £47 on your recent courses, I would be regarded as a simpleton!

What to do about this? The only practical way of going about the task of convincing the clergy is for you to undergo a complete audit of your finances by a recognised chartered accountant; this would present a total picture of your financial position, income and expenses, property, assets etc. Should you be willing to go down this road, I would ask you to discuss the matter with Father Jack McCabe.

I have decided to launch in a small way a fund to assist priests accused of child sexual abuse. Last September, you may remember, when I was leaving for the USA, on the occasion of my visiting you in hospital in Dun Laoghaire, you were kind enough to put an envelope into my pocket. When I arrived in London and opened the envelope I was amazed to discover that in your generosity you had given me £1,000. This was far too generous of you. It is my custom to use gifts given to me in this way to assist various charitable causes, and your kind gift has enabled me to launch this week, however modestly, a fund to assist priests accused of child sexual abuse.

I have today asked Father McCabe to give you £500 as a once off ex-gratia payment from this fund. This will allow you and us time to conduct the audit, should you decide to have this done, to draw up the guidelines and to address your request in a more orderly manner.

On this great feast of Easter it is my prayer that the joy of the Risen Christ will be with you.

On 3 May the bishop wrote again, saying he hoped Fortune had received the good news by then from Fr McCabe that he was to receive a maintenance allowance of £150 per week until further notice. Dr Comiskey also wrote, apparently in response to something Fortune had written in an earlier letter, about the allegations against him.

Finally, and this should be a source of assurance for you, I have never heard you state of CSA [child sexual abuse] charges against you other than that:

a) you were innocent, and,

b) you would honour your and my word of assurance to the gardaí to make yourself available when called upon. That is, at no time did you ever suggest that you were other than innocent, or that you would do anything which might suggest that you were anything other than innocent.

Finally with requests from journalists for an interview, I think it would be wise to act on the advice of your lawyers.

God's continued blessing on your priestly life and ministry, Sean.

Fortune was unhappy with the amount of money on offer and clearly felt that he was becoming increasingly isolated. He may have been toying with the notion of escape when he contacted the gardaí that year and asked them for the return of his passport, saying he wanted to travel to Rome for the beatification of the founder of the Christian Brothers, Ignatius Rice. He was told he would have to make an application to the courts.

By an interesting coincidence, during his first few remands in court, Fortune shared some of his court appearances at Wexford District Court with his old colleague from St Peter's College, Fr Donal Collins. The two priests would sit together in the courtroom.

A Message from Heaven

In 1998 Collins was sentenced to four years in prison for indecent assault and gross indecency against schoolboys. All the offences had taken place in St Peter's, with the exception of one of gross indecency which occurred in a guesthouse in Ballsbridge in Dublin, where the priest was staying with a group of students. During the court case it was revealed that Collins had not used violence against the boys, but had manipulated them into doing what he wanted. He told one boy, for example, that he would be expelled from the school if he told anyone about what he was doing to him. At the time of his sentencing, the priest made an apology to his victims, which was read out in court:

> I have behaved badly to these former pupils of mine and betrayed the trust that was given to me. At the time I had no idea of the effect such actions would cause. Through the help of a counsellor and others I have come to realise these actions brought hurt. I want to take this opportunity of making a sincere apology to them for the pain and trauma I brought into their lives. I also want to apologise to other persons to whom I have also owed a duty of trust which I failed to fulfill, especially my family, relatives, fellow workers and friends.

As the Fortune case dragged on, his victims looked to this case and wondered whether the day would ever arrive that they would receive a similar apology from their abuser. But as Collins was sent to serve his prison sentence, Fortune continued to battle and use the legal system to his advantage. His resolve was no doubt strengthened after a visit to the Curragh Prison to see Collins. He did not like what he saw there.

A year after Collins was jailed his sentence was reviewed. The court was told that he was a broken man. He was in poor health, suffering from heart problems and a muscular wasting condition. His eyesight had deteriorated badly.

Three of the four years were suspended. His age and infirmity were obvious contributors to the sentence reduction. He was freed.

From the time the allegations were made, Fortune always insisted that the case was a conspiracy against him. He said he was being blackmailed and would claim that Bishop Comiskey was insisting that he fight the case all the way to the Supreme Court, and if the judgement were to go against him there he should bring the case to Europe. His first step had been to take a judicial review of the case to the High Court, where he asserted that he could not get a fair trial because of the length of time which had elapsed between the time when the offences were allegedly committed and the date that the complaints were made. He also maintained that there had been excessive pre-trial publicity which had prejudiced his constitutional right to a fair trial, and he asserted that being charged with sixty-six criminal offences constituted an abuse of the jurisdiction of the court and was "oppressive and unjust", making the preparation of a proper defence impossible.

In May 1995, while planning his legal campaign, Fortune attended psychologist Don Lydon, a Fianna Fáil senator, for a full psychological assessment. On this occasion the information which Fortune shared on his background and his sexuality was considerably different from what he said on the previous occasions when he had been assessed.

"Fr Fortune is a man who has been living a rather erratic lifestyle for many years and has been in trouble in one way or other for many years. His family also manifests many difficulties. His father, who was a forester, died of coronary thrombosis in 1970. His mother, who had been hospitalised in St Senan's with what Fr Fortune described as hypomania, died of an overdose in 1975. She was forty-five years of age and he was around nineteen or twenty and he said that this had a devastating effect on him," said the report.

Fortune spoke of difficulties in his family as a result of his mother's illness. He told how he had been referred to Monsignor E. Feichim O'Doherty in March 1981, four months prior to being appointed to Fethard, and again in February the following year because of "the reaction of parishioners to my erratic and hypomanic behaviour". The monsignor's observations were not available to Lydon. "Since that time, however, he has been seen by a number of psychologists, psychiatrists and other medical specialists."

In addition to psychological problems, said the report, the priest had sustained physical trauma to his head. On the first occasion, in 1970, while at the Christian Brothers juniorate, he was admitted to a hospital after receiving a severe blow to the head when he accidentally hit off scaffolding. He said he was unconscious afterwards.

"I don't like admitting this, since that time I felt I was not in touch with reality. For many years after, I had occasional severe head pains but I was afraid to tell anyone about them."

In December 1984, while in Fethard, he was involved in a car crash and hospitalised. He said that he lost his memory at the time and that his brother, who had seen him on the evening of the crash, told him he had been very high.

In November 1991 there was another crash when, he said, he was again "very high" and his car turned over twice. He refused to go to hospital but did see a doctor who reported that he had "sustained injuries largely to his head alone". The doctor said that he must have been rendered unconscious as he had retrograde amnesia for a period immediately afterwards and for some days after. In fact, he told the doctor, he could not remember the details of his ordination and was vague about a great many other events. He resolutely refused to go to hospital for observation and further investigations such as skull x-rays. Between 1995 and 1997, he said he had a further four car crashes. In one of these he reported that he had been "feeling very elated and headed out into the snow and crashed", although friends had told him he was foolish to go out at that time.

Carrying out tests on Fortune, the psychologist found that his verbal scale IQ was in the bright normal range, his performance scale IQ was in the lower extreme of the dull normal range and his full scale IQ was in the average range. A "significant imbalance" existed between his verbal and performance IQ, possibly pointing to some organic factors involved in the apparent imbalance, but which Lydon found was more likely due to psychological factors.

However, other test results were "strongly suggestive" of some degree of organic damage. "In other words, a number of Fr Fortune's test results were suggestive of some degree of organic involvement and it is for this reason that I suggest that he have a brain scan." The priest had an MRI scan at the Blackrock Clinic in July 1995, but there was no evidence of organic damage. "The fact that the MRI scan was clear does not of itself outrule subtle neurological damage or deficits which could result in, for example, impulsively [sic] and poor concentration," said the report.

> Personality testing showed that Fr Fortune has specific ego weaknesses and demonstrates a resistance to change and a potential for confusion and disruption in situations that make more than average demands. There was evidence of a lack of conscious control of feelings and impulses in someone who is narcissistic and tends to have little interest in the motivation of others.

> His test results show that he was most unwilling to admit to even minor weaknesses or failings and that he was very eager to present a good front. Test results also showed evidence of over-controlled hostility, in other words, he has a tendency not to respond to aggression even appropriately most of the time, but occasionally exaggerated response of aggression may occur. All his test results show ego defensiveness and show that he is

concerned with giving a good or favourable impression and he is concerned about how others react to him.

He has strong needs for attention and affection from others and fears that these needs will not be met if he is more honest about his feelings and attitudes. He does in fact express naively optimistic and trusting attitudes toward other people and he presents himself as trusting also. He states he has high moral standards and denies hostility and negative impulses.

His test results also show that he is observant, quick, perceptive, talkative, resourceful and changeable. He is rebellious towards rules, restrictions and constraints and is generally out-going, enterprising, competitive and forward.

In relationships he would more than likely be dominant, confident, persistent, persuasive and verbally fluent. He could be described as active, forceful, ascendant and self-seeking.

The priest had initially been guarded about his sexual orientation but said he was homosexual and that his fantasy life would revolve around homosexual rather than heterosexual fantasies. "He claims to have no memory whatsoever of any of the incidents with which he has been charged but is adamant about one thing and that is that he never indulged in buggery."

Concluding, the report said that firstly there was no evidence to suggest that Fortune was psychotic. Secondly, while his MRI scan was clear, it was still possible that some minor organic deficits might exist.

But these, in my opinion, would not be sufficient to account for any of his erratic behaviour or his memory difficulties. Thirdly, there is clear evidence that he is at times extremely agitated and hypomanic. Finally, I would agree with Dr John Cooney [former consultant psychiatrist at St Patrick's Hospital in Dublin who had assessed Fortune in the mid 1980s] that Fr Fortune has indeed an unstable personality and is subject to hypomanic mood swings. These appear to be extremely severe and there is evidence that when he is "high" he gets into trouble both in his personal and with his public life.

Whether or not these hypomanic mood swings are part of a manic depressive illness I am not sure but in view of the strong family history of the illness it seems very likely, and I would rely on the conclusions of Dr Peter Fahy, whom I understand Fr Fortune has been attending for some time.

It was clear to Lydon that Fr Fortune would benefit from spiritual guidance with regard to his vocation, which might include psychosexual counselling, as well as from psychiatric help with his personality problems and hypomanic episodes. "In my opinion, this would be an ongoing process of some considerable duration."

Dr Peter Fahy was a consultant psychiatrist at the Blackrock Clinic whom Fortune began attending in 1995. In his report on the priest, Dr Fahy said that when Fortune had come to him for treatment, he had said that there were allegations that he had sexually abused a number of young people although he had not yet been charged. He was quite adamant that he had no recollection whatsoever of having abused anybody.

Dr Fahy said he felt that if he started to inquire into an aspect of Fortune's behaviour which he told him he was innocent of, approaching the case by taking a detailed history and inquiry into his background and making an attempt to establish whether or not he had committed these offences, he would delay the case. He advised that it would be in Fortune's interest to treat him along behavioural medicine lines, to decondition him to any form of abuse of others, particularly young people, using aversion therapy. Fortune agreed. In addition to inducing an aversion to abuse, said Dr Fahy, it would also help Fortune to deal with the other problems in his life and reduce his stress levels. In his report written three years after he first met the priest, Dr Fahy said that as far as he could see the course of treatment, with which he was persisting, was succeeding.

Fortune told the doctor that he had episodes of depression, during which he had a broken sleep pattern. The doctor taught him relaxation techniques which he said he practised assiduously, and later he said there was a considerable improvement in him and that he felt he had acquired the ability to avoid abuse. Dr Fahy noticed that he was rather subdued and spoke more slowly. He appeared to be depressed. He said he had had a gall bladder operation and had lost three stone in weight. Dr Fahy's record of his own opinion at that time was that Fortune was telling him the truth.

At an appointment in December 1995 (Fortune had appeared on the charges in Wexford District Court the previous month), the doctor found that he had become even more depressed. "My notes indicate that I considered him to be 'quite suicidal'. . . He admitted to feelings that life was not worth living and he had a suicidal plan that I did not think was fully formulated." The doctor prescribed further, stronger anti-depressants. In spite of the pressure, Dr Fahy wrote, Fortune had succeeded in passing significant examinations.

Dr Fahy said it was clear from his notes that he had been considering admitting the priest to a psychiatric unit. He wanted to have a second opinion, because of the gravity of the case, by an expert in the field, but unfortunately this did not work out.

Fortune continued to be depressed and his anxiety levels rose because of the stress of the impending court case. After seeing his patient in May 1996, Dr Fahy said that again the priest said that he felt life was not worth living. In April 1997 Fortune was quite distressed after learning that, from a technical point of view, he might have to plead guilty when he was in a situation where he did not believe he was guilty and had no recollection of molesting anybody. He continued to use the tape that Dr Fahy had made to reinforce his aversion to molestation.

"It was clear to me that Fr Fortune was most anxious to have help and it is important to remind oneself that he came forward spontaneously for help and did not approach me out of duress," said the report.

Dr Fahy said he had read of the investigation into his patient. He had also read the letters of various institutions and individuals which were very positive in the priest's favour. He was aware of the family history of psychological upset and agreed with the general conclusions of Don Lydon's report and the report by Monsignor O'Doherty.

Dr Fahy realised he had seen his patient in a hypomanic state on a number of occasions. He did not know of evidence that people lost their memory during a hypomanic phase:

> But in this case, in my opinion, there is a strong possibility that Fr Fortune may have been in a hypomanic phase when the alleged molestations occurred. Their insights into the seriousness of their actions, and their ability to resist a temptation to act would be weakened, and particularly during the "high" phases would be very difficult to control...
>
> Having gone to an intensive course of aversion therapy where molestation is concerned, and having attended regularly for counselling and complied with medication I am of the opinion that he is very unlikely to offend again if he has offended. I mention the latter, because I personally have not got any hard evidence that would justify me making a diagnosis of Fr Fortune being a child molester along strict, scientific, biological lines. I regret that I cannot give a more accurate opinion to the Court at this stage, and should not be surprised if other factors emerge over the next two years, which would enable me to give a more helpful approach.

He concluded by recommending in-patient observation, monitoring and treatment at St Edmundsbury Hospital. In a subsequent letter written in February 1998, Dr Fahy outlined his patient's problems and said that "his personality and manic depression cast a serious doubt, in my opinion, over his fitness to plead".

In further preparation for the case, Fortune, as well as collecting references from various people attesting to his good character, was gathering other material and even writing his own references. In the following note, he listed what he saw as his "pastoral achievements" as a priest:

1   Absolute respect for his superiors in the seminary, his Bishops – Dr Herlihy and Dr Comiskey.
2.   Dedicated to his pastoral duties, prayers and mass.
3.   Created hundreds of jobs for people amounting to almost one million pounds.
4.   Refurbishment of two parochial houses – to the point of paying out of his own pocket to the tune of £40,000 (over many years).
5.   Highly respected teachers and excellent behaviour while teaching at Palmerstown Community School, Dunlaoire Community College – as per both references from principals – attached. Also high respect by former RTE chief Bil Keating as per letter to Bishop Comiskey.
6.   Thanks expressed for his good works as per letters in 1987 [when he left Fethard] and in 1995 [when he left Ballymurn] from his Bishop.
7   Highly appreciated by students as per references.
8.   Rebuilding of schools, halls etc. His devotion to the marginalised such as his work to rehabilitate drug addicts, the sick, and old and young.
9.   His work for the local Christian Media Trust in radio broadcasting and South East Radio.
10. Fr Fortune set up the first adult education connecting

the Maynooth University and his own diocese. Nearly 200 people qualified as a result.

11. He has been very much involved in the work of Tidy Towns and community development, where his leadership led to great success.

12. Many know that he was generous to the poor, or those in any need, especially the travelling community.

Just before Christmas 1997 the judgement in the judicial review of Fortune's case was delivered by Mr Justice Geoghegan. It was to be an unpleasant seasonal gift for Paul Molloy. In essence, the twenty-eight charges relating to Paul, either indecent assault or procuring commission of an act of gross indecency, allegedly committed between 1 September 1981 and 31 August 1984, were excluded from the case. The judgement addressed the "dominion" of abusers over their victims, which may continue despite a lapse of time. There was no doubt that at the time of the alleged offences Paul would have been under the dominion of the priest, it said. However, Paul had made the decision to report the matter to Fr Devereux, Fortune's replacement in the parish, and he had built up a good relationship with the new priest. The judgement said this made it hard to see how he could still have been under the dominance of Fortune. If he had been advised not to report the matter to the gardaí by Fr Devereux and had instead reported it to the Church, that may have explained his delay in reporting the matter, but it was not attributable to Fortune's offences.

So Mr Justice Geoghegan said the time lag between the alleged offences and the prosecution was, *prima facie*, excessive and, in the absence of some cause attributable to the applicant himself, "The Applicant [Fortune] should not as a matter of fair procedure face a trial so long after the events. In this particular case, unlike other cases that I have examined in this application, the dominion cannot be said to have survived the build up of the good relationship between the new curate, Fr D [Devereux], and P.M. [Paul Molloy]."

The judge said that in the case of all the others, he was satisfied that the priest had not discharged the onus on him of showing that natural dominance, which he would have had from his position, did not continue so as to impede reporting.

On the question of pre-trial publicity, the judge said there was no doubt there had been much publicity, but he did not believe it had prejudiced the priest's constitutional right to a fair trial. Addressing the issue of the large number of charges, the judge said that by excluding Paul Molloy there would be an automatic reduction in the charges.

The decision shattered Paul Molloy. It had already taken almost two years to get this far. His decision as a teenager to go to the Church and not the gardaí to complain about his abuse had not only had no result as far as he was concerned, but now it had been used to exclude him from the case. It was at that point he decided to take a civil action against Fortune, Bishop Comiskey and the papal nuncio in Ireland.

Against legal advice, Fortune insisted that he wanted to appeal the judgement to the Supreme Court. He changed solicitors from Garrett Sheehan and Co. to local Wexford solicitor Sean Lowney. It is not known whether the Dublin firm was paid for their services. Fortune said he had sent the £40,000 bill on to the diocese, claiming that the only money he had was the £150 he received per week from the bishop. When Mr Lowney took over the case, he applied for legal aid and it was granted. As Fortune was making his appeal to the Supreme Court, the director of public prosecutions cross-appealed, in an effort to have Paul Molloy's case reinstated. Detective Garda Pat Mulcahy found himself contacting the young men involved in the case to say there would be yet another delay because of the decision to appeal. *Would it never end*, they asked him.

Fortune began appearing steadily more infirm in public. He would walk slowly with the aid of crutches and was sometimes seen in a wheelchair. He would fall asleep in the middle of conversations. He complained to doctors of widespread pains and constant fatigue and said he had difficulties with his memory.

In the North the RUC were keeping an eye on the long-drawn-out proceedings. The young man who had been abused by Fortune when he was a twelve-year-old scout in Belfast was now living in the south and had come forward during the garda investigation. The director of public prosecutions ruled that since the alleged abuse had occurred in Belfast, the RUC should be notified.

RUC officers had compiled a file concerning the reported abuse of three children. They saw from the statements that he used methods of selection and abuse similar to those which had emerged in cases of other paedophile clergy on both sides of the border, some of whom Fr Fortune knew. None of the clergy concerned has ever admitted to sharing information or victims.

The complaints against Fortune were received from children who attended the Scouts and a local youth club. Detectives interviewed most of the people who had been involved in these groups as children when the priest was in Belfast, and three made specific and serious abuse complaints against him, dating from 1979. The RUC's plan was to seek Fortune's extradition after any jail sentence served by him in the south had been completed, and accordingly RUC officers had travelled to Wexford in July 1996 to question the priest. The knowledge of their intention to extradite him made him doubly determined to delay his trial in the Republic.

The Supreme Court appeal was heard one morning in December 1998. The reasons why the charges relating to Paul Molloy should be reinstated as part of the case were presented by the director of public prosecutions, while

Fortune's counsel argued against it. Earlier the priest had dropped his own appeal to the Supreme Court. Unusually for this whole saga there was a speedy conclusion. That afternoon the chief justice, Mr Liam Hamilton, said the state's appeal had been successful and Paul Molloy's case was back in. The reasons for the decision would be delivered at a later date. This approach was being adopted so that the priest's trial should proceed without further delay.

It finally felt as if something were about to happen.

Chapter 13

"It's Not Us that Need to be Scared Today"

It was impossible to keep your eye from straying around the room that morning, trying to mark out which of the young men gathered in the courtroom were the eight involved in the case. Which were the ones who had been abused by Fr Sean Fortune?

Some sat inside the court, others stood outside. All of an age, they were young men now. That day they were flanked by mothers, fathers, sisters, brothers, partners. Was it the first time that some from Fethard had set eyes on others since they were young boys in the 1980s? Had they always thought that they were the only ones? What was it like being in such close quarters to their abuser? Paul Molloy had heard the names of some others mentioned but had never been definite about who else was involved in the case.

"It was comforting in a way to see. Some were a little more open to talk about it, but you could see that some really didn't want to be there."

The scene was unfolding in Wexford Circuit Court on Tuesday, 2 March 1999. The case was finally going ahead.

The courtroom was packed. Over seventy prospective jurors mingled with those involved in the case. Gardaí lined the side walls, and at the top table journalists vied with solicitors and barristers for possession of the few chairs available. In the few days preceding the trial, the usual slew of rumours that Fortune seemed to attract began circulating, chief among them that he would assert his constitutional right to have the case heard in Irish.

The defendant arrived at the courthouse in a wheelchair. He was assisted by his housekeeper and used crutches while climbing the stairs. "I shouldn't be here at all," he said to people as he passed. A bizarre photograph would appear in the *Wexford People* the following week, showing him inside the courthouse with one crutch on the ground and the other in the air as he held up a black umbrella to shield his face. It was funny and pathetic all at the same time.

He sat in an anteroom and had discussions with his legal team. It would be his final effort to fight the charges. His brother hovered. The small group sat and discussed last minute tactics. Yet again he told them that the charges against him were a conspiracy. As was his habit, he began to weigh up the odds: "If x happens what will be my chances of prison then? Sixty/forty, seventy/thirty? What do you think?" he would ask.

He was advised that while he might believe the case against him was a conspiracy, the impact of eight statements, each telling a similar story, would weigh heavily with a judge. That Tuesday morning he had finally come face to face with his accusers and the end of the road as far as his efforts to avoid the legal system were concerned.

Inside the courtroom time was passing. There was a constant din of noise, which would occasionally drop if people felt something were about to happen. But it didn't. At one point it was simply the court registrar coming out to get a pen. At the media table there was speculation that the absence of Fortune's senior counsel, Barry White SC, meant that nothing substantial was going to happen that day. A close eye was kept on Detective Garda Pat Mulcahy in an effort to try and get some indication of what was going on as he made his way in and out, chatting to the various parties. Two solicitors representing the Diocese of Ferns were present, there to keep a watching brief.

In fact, White had been unable to make it to the court because of a case in Dublin, which had run over from the previous day. His absence, understandably, made Fortune very anxious. "Where's Barry?" he kept asking. He wondered would it be a good idea to plead insanity. At one point, a submission was put before the presiding judge, Joseph Mathews, by the priest's counsel Jeremy Maher that the eight cases be tried separately. It was refused.

The crux of it all really was the buggery charge. Sent forward from the District Court on sixty-six charges, Fortune was to be arraigned that morning on twenty-nine of those charges. The most serious of those was a charge of buggery relating to Colm O'Gorman.

There was a suggestion that if this charge were dropped, Fortune would plead guilty to the remaining charges. Colm, who was sitting nervously in another room, knew that Fortune was attempting to make the best of his increasingly bad lot. He was asked how he would feel if the charge was dropped. His answer was a definite "No".

"The cynicism of it," recalls Colm. "One minute he was on crutches, in a wheelchair, unable to stand. The next thing he was working out how he could wriggle out of the whole thing. I needed to make him face that. It just didn't seem right to let him walk away from it. That is what happened. All I ever wanted from that court case was to be able to say what happened and to have a reaction from the justice system, and from society, an acknowledgement of it. I wanted to say that it happened."

The entire set-up seemed inappropriate, horribly reminiscent of the prelude to a compensation case involving a county council and a plaintiff who was claiming damages after falling into a pothole. What must it have been like for those boys who had been abused and had already waited so long?

Surprisingly though, for some at least the wait was not a bad thing. That morning was theirs, as one described it, and Fortune was now the one squirming. The previous few weeks had been tense. As the court day approached, the importance of coming forward and making a statement was summed up by one young man who had been abused by Fortune some years earlier.

"It still hurts to write but I know that if I don't that many other boys and girls might suffer at the hands of people like Father Fortune. Everything must be done to give Father Fortune a fair trial or hearing, but he must be brought to justice for what he has done to me and to many others. I am not a revengeful person but I do know that when people do wrong they must be man and woman enough to realise their mistake and take responsibility for their actions. I would appeal again that this enquiry must be done in the most just way and to make sure that if he is to be charged it is for the right reasons and not just to get him convicted."

Don remembers being very nervous that day, with conflicting emotions about it all. "The waiting was nerve-racking, but once I saw him I felt grand. It was the anticipation. It was knowing that I was responsible for him being there that made me feel guilty as hell. I felt that if I had not said what had happened to my dad he would not be there. Pat [Mulcahy] told me that no matter what happened, even if he pleaded guilty, I would get my say in court."

Eventually, after two and a half hours, there was some movement. Fortune made his way painfully into the room, leaning heavily on the crutches. A few days earlier neighbours in New Ross had seen him up a ladder checking the security cameras on the outside of his home, but that day his progress was torturous. He wore clerical garb, with a pioneer pin on his lapel and a gold ring on his right hand. A pair of small, round sunglasses made it impossible to see his eyes. He came to a stop close to the front of the room and slowly lowered himself on to the wooden bench. Those already sitting there struggled to make room. They were clearly uncomfortable.

When Judge Joseph Mathews came on to the bench, it apparently took great effort for Fortune to stand. The judge apologised for keeping everyone waiting for so long without, as he said, knowing why. He explained that certain applications had been made to him, the trial judge, by counsel, which were purely to do with the law and not matters for any jury. These matters had taken longer than anticipated.

He proceeded to explain what jury service involved: "You will be his judges as his fellow citizens." After the jury selection was complete, those prospective jurors who were not to be involved in the case left the courtroom, and the court registrar began the arraignment. Once again the priest struggled to stand.

"Are you Sean Fortune?" asked the court registrar.

"I am *Father* Sean Fortune," he replied, stressing the title.

The charges were read into the record, beginning with those relating to Colm O'Gorman. As each charge was read out, Fortune replied, "Not guilty." Between the sixteenth and seventeenth charges, as those relating to Paul Molloy were about to be read out, Fortune told the judge that he was getting very weak and asked if he could please sit down. The judge assented. Of the twenty-nine charges, one related to buggery, twelve to gross indecency and sixteen to indecent assault, all taking place in County Wexford between June 1981 and December 1987.

Afterwards Colm said he would always remember that particular moment. "Having those charges read out in court – it was an incredible moment. I was not scared going into the court. I just thought, "This is my day, I'm not scared today. It's not us that need to be scared today. It was a long four years, not knowing what was going on."

At the outset Fortune's counsel, Jeremy Maher, told the court that a witness for the priest was not available. The man lived in England and was currently on holidays in Greece. He applied for the case to be adjourned until the next sitting. After some discussion the request was denied, with Judge Mathews pointing out that it had been a number of years since the case had been returned for trial in the court, so arrangements could have been easily made. Prosecuting counsel Michael Counihan SC pointed out that the state had, at great difficulty and expense, flown in witnesses from the US, Germany, England and Spain.

Mr Maher then spoke about the physical condition of his client, saying that he was under treatment from a number of doctors, one of whom had prescribed morphine. There was concern, he said, about his capacity to participate in a trial. As he spoke his client sat with his head resting on the bench in front of him, looking as if he had fallen asleep. It was an incongruous sight. A garda approached, shook him gently, and asked if he was all right.

Judge Mathews listened to the submissions, and the jurors who had just been sworn in were told they could go home for the rest of the day. After some thought, he said another jury would have to be sworn in to hear expert medical evidence on Fortune's fitness to plead in the case. Since the scores of prospective jurors who had not been selected had been sent home earlier in the day, it would not now be possible to organise new candidates for another three weeks. If, when they heard the medical evidence, the new jury decided Fortune was fit, a third set of jurors would then have to be found to hear the case. Just when it had all seemed so close, it was slipping away again.

In the afternoon, submissions continued on the state of the priest's physical and mental health. The court heard evidence from the consultant psychiatrist, Dr Peter Fahy, who had been treating Fortune in the years before the trial. Ironically, Dr Fahy had not been due to attend the court until the next day, but a mix up in dates meant that he was available on that day to give evidence of Fortune's condition. At one point in the proceedings, Judge Mathews, on a point of law, made a passing reference to another case which happened to be a murder trial. A short time later Fortune, giving direct evidence of his ill health, announced to the judge that he felt he was being charged with murder.

"Did I murder anyone, Pat?" he asked, looking at Pat Mulcahy who was sitting across from him. "Tell the judge, Pat," he urged, before it was explained to him that this was not indeed the charge he was facing.

Judge Mathews told Fortune that he was sending him for treatment and assessment to the Central Mental Hospital (CMH), Dundrum. This was certainly not the outcome the priest had wanted or expected. At best he would have been found unfit; if there were only an adjournment, he wanted to remain on bail. Afterwards, as he waited to be taken away, he complained bitterly to his legal team about the decision. He said he would continue with psychiatric treatment on his own, as he had been doing. He stood, waiting to be taken away, clearly unhappy. He handed over the money he had with him to his housekeeper.

At any one time there are a handful of people in the CMH who have been sent there as a result of having been found unfit to plead in criminal proceedings. However, Fortune never made it to the CMH, but was sent instead to Mountjoy Prison in Dublin. It was widely reported at the time that the reason was a strike involving SIPTU care workers at the hospital. Maureen Browne, spokeswoman for the Eastern Health Board, has since said that this was not the reason.

"The story went around that it was because of the strike, but that was not the case. If you are going to the CMH there are legislative procedures laid down because it is a hospital and not a jail. He was brought to Mountjoy and when he arrived there the psychiatrist examined him to see if he should be referred to the Central Mental Hospital. It was decided that he should not."

Mountjoy was Fortune's first experience of being incarcerated and he hated it, even though on arrival there he was put in a room by himself in the medical centre where conditions are far better that in the ordinary cells.

The next day the jury which had been sent home just twenty-four hours earlier gathered again at Wexford courthouse to be told by Judge Mathews that it had become apparent from submissions that the priest was unwell and he had sent him to hospital.

"He felt that I, as a judge, was charging him with murder," he told a surprised jury before discharging them.

After five nights in Mountjoy Prison, Fortune was back in court the following Monday. Dressed in a black leather jacket, with the ever-present shades covering his eyes, he appeared before the then Mr Justice Cyril Kelly in the High Court to seek bail. The judge was told that because of the dispute at the CMH the priest had been kept at Mountjoy. He had only been medically examined once while there. It was ironic that he would appear before Mr Justice Kelly. In a matter of weeks, he and Judge Mathews would be central characters in what became known as the Sheedy affair. Judge Cyril Kelly gave an early release to Philip Sheedy, an architect who had been convicted of causing the death by dangerous driving of a young Dublin mother, who had earlier been jailed for four years by Judge Mathews. The Supreme Court judge Mr Justice Hugh O'Flaherty also became embroiled in the case. He and Kelly subsequently resigned.

That day Judge Kelly heard that Fortune had been on bail for most of the time since he was first charged and had always honoured that bail. When they objected to the bail, the gardaí did not object on the usual grounds that a defendant might interfere with witnesses or that they feared he might abscond; they simply wanted him psychiatrically assessed and treated, as previously ordered.

"It's Not Us that Need to be Scared Today"

In contrast to his court appearance the previous week, Fortune was lucid and able to respond without difficulty to the judge when asked if he understood what bail was and what an independent surety meant. He gave a guarantee that he would comply with anything ordered by the court and make himself available for any psychiatric assessment.

Judge Kelly granted bail on the priest's undertaking that he would attend medical examinations organised on behalf of the state. He was also directed to sign on once a week at a garda station. The bail was granted on Fortune's own surety of £5,000, and an independent surety of the same amount paid by his brother.

After the hearing, Fortune told his legal team that he was in considerable physical pain and a lot of his pills were missing. He said he had made an appointment to see his own psychiatrist. Leaving them, he was brought back to Mountjoy to collect his belongings and was released that evening.

Looking back, Don says he reckons that Fortune finally realised at that stage that the game was up. "John used his head to get out of things and he was trying whatever way he could to manipulate the situation. I think that is what happened that day in Wexford court – he realised he could not work his way out – his threats or his intelligence would not work. I thought at one stage he would back down and plead guilty and do the intelligent thing. If you bring a con that far and if it does not work, you accept second best and try and get the most from that. He could have tried to show himself in a sympathetic light, in terms of a psychological report, and throw himself at the mercy of the courts. I guess he was aware of what happens to people like him in prison."

If he had been given the opportunity to take the stand and tell the court how the abuse had affected him, Don said he would have told the priest, whom he had known for over half his life, that it was something he had to do. "I would have said, 'John, this is nothing personal, what I am doing to you. The fact is that you are a danger to society, you were not going to address the problem, so the only way to address it is to take you away from society. I was not out for revenge.'"

It can hardly be imagined what it must have been like for this man who loved the spotlight to be caught under its glare for an offence such as sexual abuse. The priest who had once been the pride of his family had now brought them great shame and there was worse to come. Two Irish priests have been dismissed from the clerical state within the past seven years for offences of sexual abuse. According to the Catholic Press Office in Dublin, they cannot be named, by order of the courts, to protect the identity of victims. In the UK a fifty-six-year-old Catholic priest, Fr John Lloyd, who is serving an eight-year sentence for sex offences against children, was dismissed by papal decree in 1999. That decision by Pope John Paul II is believed to have been the first such "dismissal from the clerical state", to use the Vatican phrase, of a British priest in recent history. He was sentenced for the rape of a sixteen-year-old girl and a series of indecent assaults on two altar boys. Three priests in the US were dismissed in similar circumstances in the US in 1988.

After such a dismissal, the priests cannot conduct any church services and they are banned from teaching in a Catholic school or college. It was expected, according to the Catholic Press Office, that such a process would have been initiated against Brendan Smyth had he lived. Normally, a penalty as serious as this can only be imposed after a full canonical trial. In the instance of Lloyd, however, the pope decided to by-pass the process because of "the importance of sparing those who were hurt any further distress".

If Fortune were found guilty, such a step could hardly have been avoided by the Irish Catholic Church, and that really must have been unimaginable to him. He so loved being a priest and the privileges it brought. He clearly enjoyed the dressing up, the formality, the showmanship, the standing in the community and, last but not least, the position of trust which gave him easy access to children. It was this last feature which he shared with so many other clerical abusers. Sean Fortune was just one of a long list of Catholic priests to come before the Irish courts in recent years. The Catholic Church introduced guidelines on how to deal with allegations of sexual abuse in January 1996. Fr Martin Clarke of the Catholic Press Office says that prior to the introduction of these guidelines cases were dealt with on an individual basis within the twenty-six dioceses covering the island of Ireland and the 200 religious congregations within that which would have had a measure of autonomy. "They would have dealt with the issue within each diocese or congregation," says Fr Clarke. The press office keeps a tally of the number of sex abuse cases involving priests. From 1983 to July 2000 almost fifty priests have been convicted of such offences, the majority in the Republic and the remainder in the North. The list includes diocesan priests who served in Ireland, diocesan priests serving abroad, former diocesan priests, religious order priests, religious order brothers, former religious order priests and ex-religious brothers. As the figures show, there were many individuals who used the Church as a cloak for their distorted desires.

The name Brendan Smyth is the one that first comes to mind for most Irish people when they think of priests who have abused. Smyth was seventy when he collapsed and died in prison at the Curragh in August 1997 while serving a sentence related to abuse he carried out in the Republic. The manner in which his and other cases, including Fortune's, were dealt with indicates a much larger malaise within the Church. The Dublin priest Fr Ivan Payne was sentenced to two years in prison in June 1998 after pleading guilty to thirteen sample charges of sexual assaults on teenage boys which began in 1968 when he was appointed chaplain at Our Lady's Hospital for Sick Children in Crumlin, Dublin, and continued until 1987. Payne spent time in Canada in the early 1970s, but in 1976 he returned to Ireland and was appointed to the Dublin Archdiocese's Regional Catholic Marriage Tribunal which dealt with marriage annulments. He also became chaplain at Cabra, where he was until 1981 when he was removed from his post after a complaint was made against him by Andrew Madden who had served as an altar boy there. Following treatment by a psychiatrist, he was appointed parish chaplain in Sutton in Dublin in early 1982. The psychiatrist again saw the priest in 1991 and 1994 to review the situation. In November 1994 the story emerged in the *Irish Press* and in March 1995 Andrew Madden went public on the matter in an interview in the *Sunday World*. It was disclosed on an RTÉ "Prime Time" programme in September 1995 that in 1993 Payne had secured a loan of £30,000 from the Dublin Archdiocese to pay an out-of-court settlement to Mr Madden. In May 1995 the Archbishop of Dublin Dr Desmond Connell had told RTÉ he had paid out no compensation to any victim of clerical child sex abuse and claimed he had been libelled by "Prime Time". "To say we paid compensation is completely untrue," he said afterwards. In a statement following the hearing of Payne's case in April 1998, Dr Connell said Payne was referred to a specialist institute for residential assessment in 1995 "as a further precaution". This followed revelations about Brendan Smyth. "It was decided that Father Payne should withdraw from ministry. Thereafter, as is now well known, additional complaints came to light and the Garda investigation commenced," continued Dr Connell.

Speaking at Payne's court case, a consultant psychiatrist at the Granada Institute, which treats victims and perpetrators of sexual abuse, Marie Keenan, who began treating

Payne in 1995, described the three consultations the priest had had with the psychiatrist prior to that as totally inadequate as treatment. In his judgement, the then Judge Cyril Kelly said that Payne had been a paragon at the pinnacle of propriety cloaked in a veneer of theology. He remarked that his standing in the communities in which he served was "exactly the crux of the issue for the children. They were convinced they would not be believed."

Payne publicly apologised to all his victims from the witness box at his hearing. He said he wanted to acknowledge he had hurt many people by his behaviour, including his victims, their family and friends, as well as his own family and friends. The Catholic Church is facing civil actions from a number of men who say they were abused by Payne.

That day in March 1999 when Fortune stood in Wexford District Court and heard each charge being read out to him and faced his victims in the courtroom, he must have realised that the game was up. Looking at him, it was clear then that the enormity of the case weighed heavily on him. It was easy to react with cynicism to his stories of physical ill health, but by then it was the only tactic remaining. Desperation drove him.

He returned to his heavily guarded home in New Ross after his release from Mountjoy. Pressure had been mounting in the town, with local youths hassling and taunting him, throwing stones at his house and kicking the shutters. Shortly before his last court appearance in Wexford, he made a call to gardaí to complain of harassment by a gang of youths who had gathered outside. When the gardaí arrived, he replayed them the tape from the security camera. It showed the gang running away and himself giving chase down the street.

He did make arrangements to see his family that weekend. However, that Thursday night, 11 March 1999, he clearly saw suicide as the only way out. As seen from his medical notes, it was not the first time he had contemplated such an act. It was a tragic end for him, for his family and for his victims.

His attempt at writing out an apology for his misdeeds, in preparation for the court case, makes it clear that he was simply unwilling to face his actions and would never have been able to plead guilty. The apology, customarily read out in court prior to sentencing after a defendant has been found or pleaded guilty, was curmudgeonly to say the least. Without doubt, if the situation had arisen, his counsel would have suggested that he change it.

My Lord and members of the Court

I Fr Sean Fortune priest of the Diocese of Ferns hereby apologise with deep remorse to all those I have offended. I have no memory of these events, yes, as the Doctors pointed out, and I thank them for their professional help. Medical reasons have been given for this, which I am sure are very accurate and also it happened so long ago. But, based not on my memory but on the Statements of these young people, I must profoundly apologise to these fine young people before the Court whom I have grievesly distressed and offended by my behaviour which was wrong before God and man. Thankfully, to my doctors I am now on a course of treatment. As you know, I have been seriosly psychiatrically ill for many years and at present seriously physically ill also. Thanks be to God the probability of re-offending is highly unlikely indeed according to the Doctors. I can honestly say I meant no harm in whatever alleged harm I caused to these young people. But I know in reading their Statements and Affidavits that they have been grievesly distressed and sinned against and before my God, your Lordship and this Court I humbly apologise for this. I ask forgiveness of my dear family and my dear friend the Bishop Dr Brendan Comiskey, the Priests and people of the Diocese of Ferns and of God's holy Church. But I like St Patrick can truthfully say Ego Pecator I a sinner. I have always forgiven anybody who did my any wrong in my life whether perceived or real and I beg God's forgiveness and the forgiveness of these people for any wrong I have done them.

I thank in particular the Garda Siochana and in a special way Detective Garda Pat Mulcahy and the State for their kindness and courteosy at all times and also my legal team. I thank Alymighty God too for the spiritual counselling of my brother Priests within and without the Diocese of Ferns.

These events have greatly shattered my priestly life and physical health. Jesus said, forgive and you shall be forgiven. The forgiveness of all here present and especially of those who were sinned against and their families. To quote a leading Author, to err is human to forgive divine.

Bishop Brendan Comiskey wrote to me and my brother Priests in Ferns one Christmas recently saying "events however stressful can never overcome us, only a fearful heart, lacking in faith can do that". Let us keep our eyes fixed on Jesus and on him alone, hoping I can do that as I repent of my sinfulness towards these good people.

Finally, I ask the ladies and gentlemen of the Press, whom I worked for, for many years, to be aware of members of my family who are very ill at this present time, in the way that they ligitimaly cover this tragedy. I ask for God and Blessed Titus Brandsman the renowened Journalist of the Nazi Concentration Camp who gave his life for the truth of Journalism that you do not sensationalise but present the facts as they are before this Circuit Court of Saor Stait Eireann. I repeat my absolute apology and sincere remorse to all affected by my sinfullness whether they be living or dead. I like Oscar Wilde believe that "everything has a pasp and every sinner a future".

But Sean Fortune clearly saw no future. On the Saturday morning when she arrived at his house, found it locked up and knew there was something wrong, it was still a huge shock to Margaret Stamp to go inside with Peter Bennett and find him lying dead on the bed.

At around 1pm when he heard the news of the suicide, Don was at work. "My head was in a complete spin after the court case which had brought it all back up again, and then I had to deal with the suicide. I went home and I bawled my eyes out. I kept thinking that the whole thing just wasn't necessary. People say it was the coward's way out, but it has never been easy to kill yourself. The thing to do if you deceive people is to keep your eye on the ball; it stops working if you start believing it yourself. When confronted with it he couldn't handle it. The judge in the circuit court had him pegged from the word go. He knew he couldn't fake medical reports. All the lies were at an end. He left a terrible legacy behind him. Everyone believes us, but in the eyes of the law we will always be the alleged victims. Now I will never be able to look him straight in the eye and say, 'You did this to us.' He also did it to his family."

In the days afterwards, as the shock receded, Don remembered the Fr Fortune he had known. "He was intelligent and exceptionally bright. I'm fairly bright, but he was way ahead of me. He would have made a brilliant politician or salesman. But the choice of priest was no coincidence; they have such a central role in the community. There is no doubt that in his mind he was going to be a bishop or above it. I don't think that the abuse was a sexual thing, or at least a wholly sexual thing. He really wanted to be in control. They say that there are different types of abusers, only with a few is it purely sexual. He wanted control on every level. If you get people to submit, especially if it is against their nature, you have ultimate control.

"On a day-to-day basis the abuse does not affect me. I am a whole, well-rounded person, with no problem in the sex department. But that does not take away from the fact that I had to deal with it. I had to grow up and put it behind me and get rid of the guilt. The legacy now is a complete lack of faith. I was always questioning anyway, to see a man like Fortune and to let him get away with what he did. The bishop did go through the processes, but when you have someone like John Fortune, clearly you have to go outside the process."

Colm O'Gorman lives in London now, but he was at home in Wexford when he received the news of the suicide. The following day he was attempting to come to terms with it. "There are prayers for the family of Fr Fortune at masses today, and I am, too, I am praying for him. I wept for him. But there was no mention of the rest of us in the churches. Obviously there were other constraints, but they could have said they were also praying for the others affected. It was sad for me, my family and for all the boys who had been abused and their families, dreadfully sad. He was a human being too; the tragedy now is that he is a victim as well. The system failed for me and for him," said Colm sadly. "I think that being in Mountjoy put even more pressure on him. On one level I welcomed that, but not for it to end like this. It was not right for us or for him."

Paul Molloy was at home in the US when he received a call early that Saturday morning from his family telling him of his abuser's death. That night he said he was upset that Fortune would never be formally found guilty in a court of law.

"He will never be made sit through a trial and to hear everybody's story. I wanted to see his reaction, to see if he would show any remorse. I feel he wouldn't have. I wanted to look down on him as I told my story and to see him cringe. That won't happen now."

A year earlier Paul had instructed New Ross solicitor Simon Kennedy to proceed with a civil case against the Bishop of Ferns and the papal nuncio and Fr Fortune for damages and a declaration that they failed in their duty to him. Paul's will be the first case to go ahead, but he has since been joined by a number of the other young men involved in the criminal case, including Colm and Don.

That Sunday the newspapers carried reports of the death of the priest. As the shock wore off, attention turned to Dr Comiskey and his role in the sorry tale. The bishop, it transpired, was in the US in the run-up to St Patrick's Day. Queries were handled by his spokeswoman, Barbara Wallace, a personal friend who runs a public relations firm in Wexford. At her request, this author faxed a list of questions to the bishop on behalf of *The Irish Times* that afternoon, dealing mainly with the complaints about Fortune over the years and how the bishop had handled them. Later, in response, Wallace said that the bishop "had absolutely nothing to say about any of the matters put to him at this time". There was a "monstrous" number of files relating to Fr Fortune, "going from floor to ceiling". As Dr Comiskey would be very busy with confirmations on his return and because his secretary was sick, he would have great difficulty getting at them. As it was, he felt it would be insensitive of him, at that time, to go into any details of the man while his family was grieving and he was not yet buried. Wallace indicated that the bishop would speak later in the week.

Gathering his thoughts that day, Paul Molloy said he wanted an explanation from Dr Comiskey as to why, as he believed it, no action was taken about the sexual abuse he suffered and complained about to the Church in 1988. Colm O'Gorman felt the Church had an opportunity to put things right, and "to give leadership to people, by doing what they are supposed to do and acting with love, compassion and respect".

Then there was the matter of Fortune's obsequies. Where would he be buried? Who would say the funeral mass? Who would attend? In the note left for his family, he stated that he wanted his funeral to be held in Ballymurn. In fact his will revealed that he had very specific wishes, not just about the location, and the instructions had the usual Fortune flourishes. In the will he had made in August

1997, he asked that his remains be "brought back to Ballymurn and laid for a day and a night before the altar. My requiem mass to be held at 12 noon. It is my express wish that the Bishop for the time being of Ferns be present and preside and preach at my funeral liturgy." All other priests he said were welcome in "choral dress", soutane and surplice as worn during the high mass. It was also his wish that the Ballymurn school choir would sing at the mass and he specified the hymns, including "Sweet Heart of Jesus", the "Our Father" in Irish and "Be Not Afraid". He gave the readings and the Gospel and asked that members of his family and his housekeeper Margaret carry his breviary, his priest's stole and other the gifts in the offertory procession. He wanted to be buried beside a particular priest in the graveyard.

He also left instructions concerning what should be written on his headstone: "Here lies Father Sean Fortune, formerly c.c. Holy Rosary, Belfast, Poulfur and Ballymurn. Born 20 December 1953, became a Christian Brother 15 August 1973, Brother De Sales, ordained 27 May 1979 and departed to his Lord . . ."

That Saturday evening in Ballymurn church, local curate Fr James Kavanagh broke the news to parishioners. He asked for their support and that they attend the funeral, even though the priest had lived a life less than perfect. Catering would be needed afterwards for over 100 priests.

It was just too much for the congregation. One man got up and left the church in protest, and afterwards further protests were voiced. People felt they had hardly recovered from having Fortune as their priest without having to endure his funeral mass and burial. Without even knowing the contents of his will, there had been concerns that local children would be required to serve on the altar during the mass. Local women did not take kindly to the request for catering. The subject was not raised at masses on Sunday morning, and it was later announced that the funeral would be held in his home town of Gorey, where he would be buried alongside his parents in St Michael's Cemetery.

On Monday in response to further queries from *The Irish Times* asking when the bishop would be prepared to speak about Fr Fortune, Barbara Wallace said he had just returned from the US, he was very busy and would be unlikely to make any comment that week. That evening around 100 people attended the removal in Gorey. During those days Fr Sean Fortune was the talk of the country, but much as he loved attention, the nature of the discussions would not have pleased him. On the Radio One chat shows, listeners' opinions were divided between those who believed that it was not right to speak ill of the dead, especially before he had even been buried, and those whose sympathy lay with the victims who were robbed of their day in court.

Fr Peter O'Callaghan, of Candlemas, a group formed to comfort and support those bereaved by suicide, raised a number of pertinent issues in a letter he wrote to *The Irish Times* about the suicide:

> The suspected suicide of Father Sean Fortune, a suspended priest of the Diocese of Ferns at his home in New Ross last Saturday morning, like the natural death of the convicted paedophile Brendan Smyth while serving his prison sentence, will be contemplated with mixed feelings.
>
> For Father Fortune's family and friends, as they say a final farewell to a person and priest they loved, the days ahead will be a heartbreaking time of great sadness and grief which they will relive over and over again for many months and years. No one should intrude on their private grief. As one who shared the ministry of Catholic priesthood with Father Sean, my prayers and sympathy are very much with his family and friends at this time.

"Fr Fortune," he continued, "was before the courts on very serious charges to which he had pleaded not guilty.

"It's Not Us that Need to be Scared Today"

The charges against him – twenty-nine counts of sexual abuse – were so serious that a judge deemed it necessary to detain him in custody pending his trial." Fr O'Callaghan pointed out that from the High Court he had returned to his diocese and home to die alone by an apparent self-induced death by alcohol and medication.

> May I ask Bishop Brendan Comiskey, Father Fortune's Ordinary, what help – spiritual or other – was offered to Father Fortune (who in court was clearly a very ill man) after his release from prison in the days immediately before his death? The Roman Ritual on "The Pastoral of the Sick" declares: "The Lord himself showed great concern for the bodily and spiritual welfare of the sick and commanded his followers to do likewise."
>
> Since it seems from media reports that Father Fortune barricaded himself in his house after being released from prison, I wonder did this also place him beyond diocesan help and the spiritual support, comfort and consolation of his Church in an obvious time of illness and great personal disgrace and shame?

Fr O'Callaghan also asked the ministers for health and justice whether there had been any hint that the priest was going to commit suicide while he was in their care waiting to face a judge and jury for the acts he was accused of.

The Fortune family would also wonder why no action was taken to ensure that he could do no harm to himself. Indeed, when he had apparently been a danger to himself and others for many years, as complaints and some of the medical reports suggest, why, as far as they were concerned, was no action taken by his superiors in the Church? As Fr O'Callaghan pointed out in his letters, the questions will remain with them over many years, complicated by the allegations facing their brother at the time of his death.

Four days after he had been found dead, criminal proceedings against Fortune were formally struck out when

Judge Olive Buttimer was informed at a sitting of Wexford Circuit Court that the defendant in the case was now deceased. In Gorey that Tuesday morning, around 140 people were gathering for the funeral mass in St Patrick's Church: family, clerics and others, mainly elderly people, the majority of those women. The stalwarts who had consistently refused to lose faith in Fortune huddled together and shared their grief. The priests sat together on one side of the church, gathered together in pews. There were about twenty-four of them sitting in a reserved area which could have taken many more. Their discomfort was evident, being made worse by the large gathering of media outside the door. Their clerical garb made them obvious targets for photographers. Afterwards they were criticised for attending, but it was easy to see their dilemma. Should they stay away in solidarity with all those he hurt, or extend the Christian ethos to its limit and support the Fortune family in their time of need? Yet it was clear that they did not wish to be tainted with the actions of their former colleague. It was never going to be an easy situation. There was no pride that day in wearing priests' collars. In the town most people had mixed feelings. They did sympathise with the family, but they did not wish to attend the funeral.

When the time arrived for the homily, Dr Comiskey, returned from the US, stood and addressed the congregation. Fr Fortune's hope, he said, like that of all believers, lay in the mercy of God and God – to use that phrase of the pope's – was "rich in mercy".

At a Catholic funeral mass the Church instructed the homilist not to eulogise the dead person – meaning to speak well of someone – "but to tell the people of the Gospel of Jesus Christ, namely, the good news of God's love for him, for her, for all of us. This is to teach as Jesus did and Jesus always returned to the theme of 'Let me tell you how much the Father loves you.'" He proceeded to tell the biblical tale of the lost farthing, the lost sheep and the lost sons, as well as quoting from the poet Patrick Kavanagh.

He asked the family and friends of Fr Fortune to believe, above all at this time of sadness in their lives, in the love and mercy of God. "To lose a brother, an uncle, a friend in these tragic circumstances is especially painful. Believe, hope and trust in the mercy of God, who knows all, and forgives all." It seemed at first that there was to be no mention of the court case and Fr Fortune's victims, but as he reached his conclusion, the bishop said that there was another group of people to whom he wished to speak. Everyone was aware, because they lived in the real world, that there was a trial process underway at the time of his death. Because of the sudden nature and timing of Fr Fortune's death, this had come to a premature end.

"This development in itself adds further to the pain of all those who had looked to this particular process to alleviate their plight. I take this opportunity on behalf of the Christian community, and indeed on my own behalf, to acknowledge their pain, to ask for prayers for them that they may find some peace of mind and some healing. I recognise that because of their particular circumstances, there may be reluctance on the part of some to avail of any offer of help from the Church. Nevertheless, I once again offer the service of the diocese and my own services to help in whatever way we can. God comfort you. Hope in God, believe in him still."

Just as it sounds, the text of the bishop's sermon had been vetted and approved by diocesan solicitors. The careful yet generalised phrasing when referring to those who had been abused was well noted, as was the absence of the use of the word "victim". The bishop said that he "once again" offered the service of the diocese and his own services. The offer rang a little hollowly with the victims when contrasted with their actual experience. The previous offers of help were difficult to remember, and while the bishop was publicly calling on those hurt to come forward, his legal team was vigorously fighting the civil actions taken by victims.

Outside the church, TV cameramen and photographers waited for Dr Comiskey to come out, but the wait was in vain. He left using another exit and returned immediately to the US to fulfil his engagement to speak at a Catholic Society function as part of the St Patrick's Day celebrations. A wealthy American, the same man who had provided the funding for the diocese to become involved in local radio, was paying for all the flights. Once again Bishop Comiskey's priests faced the waiting cameras. Their hostility was even more obvious now as a number glared at reporters.

The funeral cortège made its slow way to the edge of the town. Members of the Fortune family led the mourners as they walked behind the hearse, garlanded with wreaths. At St Michael's Cemetery, the beleaguered procession came to a halt at one of the older graves. A statue of Our Lady of Lourdes with rosary beads hanging from her neck stood over a weathered white headstone, reading:

> In Loving memory of James Fortune
> Forest Cottage, Gorey
> Died 17th April 1970
> His wife Elizabeth Fortune,
> Died 5th July 1976,
> RIP

The gravel had been removed and the ground broken for the first time in over twenty years; this time it was for the remains of the couple's eldest son John, as they had known him. Afterwards the grave was refilled with earth and the brown gravel spread once more.

The father of one of the abused boys was unimpressed with events, particularly the sermon and the offer of help. "The bishop said at his press conference when he came back from America that time that he had 'cried with' families who had children abused by priests. It certainly was not us and he was told about the case of my son. What about the other boys in the Fortune case? Has he visited them?"

Two days after Fortune's funeral *The Irish Times* once again contacted Barbara Wallace seeking a response from the bishop on the different complaints made to him about Fortune's abuse of young boys – the first of those made shortly after his arrival in the Diocese of Ferns in 1984 and subsequent approaches. Additional questions were faxed to his spokeswoman involving those allegations, as well as the persistent complaints to the bishop over the years about the priest's otherwise bizarre and obnoxious behaviour.

In a responding fax, Wallace pointed out that this brought the total number of queries to Dr Comiskey to seventeen.

> We would like to help or facilitate you if and when possible, however I would reiterate the points which I made to you which preclude me from giving a firm promise as to when/if the Bishop might respond.
>
> – The queries cover many different cases, alleged incidents over a long period of time.
>
> – This would necessitate examining many files.
>
> – The Bishop's secretary is on sick leave.
>
> – The Bishop has an exceptionally busy schedule with confirmations almost every day, coming into Holy Week ceremonies, on top of his other work.
>
> I would also remind you that it may well be (I don't know) that the Bishop's legal advisors would consider it unwise to answer some of your questions while the civil action is pending.
>
> Under all of these circumstance I would repeat that personally I believe that it would be unfair to publish the list of questions and a line that says that the Bishop has not responded. As to your request from me to suggest the

bottom line – having dealt with the *Irish Times* for over 20 years, I would be surprised that they would consider it fair to publish a list such as the one submitted without awaiting the Bishop's decision as to whether or not he could supply answers.

Chapter 14

Gross Abuse of Priestly Power

As THE FALL-OUT from the revelations following Fortune's death continued, it was becoming clear that any possibility of the bishop's explaining his role, which had first been publicly questioned four years previously, was fading. That week in *The Irish Times* office, this author received calls each day from people who had been abused in some way or another by Sean Fortune. They were terribly sad stories. The worst were the young men. What could be done other than to listen to their stories and advise that they seek professional help? There was little point now in going to the gardaí. They called from different parts of the country; all had at one stage in their lives come across the priest. Some were former students from St Peter's College; others had been on holidays in Fethard or were part of a retreat or youth group that had visited there. One, now in his thirties, had been on a visit there with a church group when he woke up to find Fortune in the bed and interfering with him. It was fifteen years later, but the trauma was obviously still great.

"I keep remembering it," he said. He didn't think that counselling would be of any use. "I'm coping with it myself."

In advance of that weekend's Sunday newspapers, the bishop issued another statement, essentially maintaining the "holding pattern" of previous statements, saying that since the death of Fr Fortune he had been asked for a detailed response to a number of questions, the most grave of which concerned complaints of child sexual abuse against Fr Fortune. He wished to acknowledge again "the pain of all those who had been awaiting the outcome of the criminal proceedings against Father Fortune to provide answers".

> The impression has been given that complaints of child sexual abuse were made to me in respect of which I made no response. I am conscious of the fact that there is anxiety among those seeking answers that I put on the public record the nature of these complaints and the responses made to them. It is quite true that I received such complaints. It is untrue, however to say that I did nothing about them. There are in train High Court proceedings seeking damages in which I am one of a number of named defendants. There may be legal implications which will limit the amount of information I am free to put into the public domain before such proceedings are determined. The advice which I receive about these implications will guide the timing and content of any further statement which I may make in advance of such proceedings.

Again he offered his own services and those of the diocese "in whatever way we can" and provided the telephone number for Faoiseamh, the Church helpline. At that time there were people who felt that Dr Comiskey's statement again leant more towards that of a lawyer rather than a bishop. It was a time when they were hoping for a response from him that reflected the hurt and confusion of the situation and perhaps showed a way to heal and go forward, something that would, in a sense, transcend legalities. Added to that was the news that the papal nuncio, Dr Luciano Storero, was claiming diplomatic immunity in the civil actions being taken by Fortune's victims, under the Vienna Convention. Contacting the nuncio, who is based in Dublin, is not an easy matter. Queries, according to the woman who answered the telephone at his residence, are only accepted by fax and it would not be possible to speak to a spokesperson. In the subsequent fax, the nuncio was asked to comment on the version of events given by Kieran from Fethard-on-Sea that his predecessor Dr Alibrandi had been informed of some of the allegations against Fortune in the 1980s and to confirm that he was pleading diplomatic immunity in the civil actions. A few days later, the response from the woman on the telephone was brief. "His excellency says that he has no comment to make."

Watching it all unfold from Fethard-on-Sea, Sean Cloney was unimpressed yet again by the response from the Catholic Church. "Diplomatic immunity would, of course, be one way out, if it worked. However the papal nuncio must be aware of what has gone on in this diocese and I know his main function must be to relay information to the Vatican. But the Vatican in turn should be able to respond and to take action. History tells us that the Church is quite secretive and will not bow to outside pressure. In its time the Church will change, but a lot of suffering and pain will take place before it happens."

In the final years of his life Sean underwent great suffering following a car accident in 1995 which left him paralysed from the neck down. There had been many times when it was not expected that he would pull through, susceptible as he was to opportunistic infections. At his home in Dungulph, near Fethard, hooked up to various machines assisting him to stay alive, he was attended by twenty-four-hour nursing care.

However he showed steely determination born, one often suspected, of a need to see the Fortune case through. To anyone who met Sean, his acceptance of his condition was remarkable. He was unfailingly good-humoured and retained his excellent historian's memory for detail, backed up by the considerable archive he had built up over decades.

A Message from Heaven

Almost twenty years after Fortune came into his life, Sean remained in wonderment at the man who wreaked such havoc in their parish. "I am disappointed that he committed suicide. It leaves a big gap in the lives of the victims. I believe that even if the bishop visited the victims it would be a beginning, but he seems to have almost ignored them," said Sean, adding that they felt they had been failed by the Church.

Sean never had any hesitation in speaking out about what went on in Fethard, but his utterances, which struck many of those who heard them as brave, were often a source of exasperation to the people of the area. They wondered whether they would ever be left to get on with their lives without being reminded of the bitterness involving the Catholic Church over the years. If only Sean would let it be, then the wounds would heal, they felt. Sean was aware that there were a number who believed that he had ended up paralysed because he "went against the Church". Sadly, in October 1999, at the age of seventy-three, he died, less than a year after the death of his daughter Mary.

In a tribute to Sean, published in the *Sunday Independent*, Ronan Fanning, professor of modern history at UCD, remembered how Sean had taken him quietly aside during a holiday in Fethard in 1984 and suggested that if he wanted to take his children to mass that he should go to Templetown rather than Poulfur, where Fortune was priest.

"I remember too seeing Fortune strutting through the summer sunshine in Fethard in his soutane, looking the very epitome of a sleek, proud prelate in embryo."

Professor Fanning felt it would have been fitting for an apology given by Bishop Comiskey for the Fethard boycott to have been reaffirmed at Sean's funeral mass:

> . . . but Bishop Comiskey, alas, did not attend. I am glad, too, that Sean Cloney lived to see the release of "A Love Divided", the compelling film which tells the story of the boycott, albeit in a slightly fictionalised form.

But "A Love Divided" identifies what lay at the heart of the Fethard-on-Sea boycott: the gross abuse of priestly power – that priestly power that Sean Fortune was to abuse to different and even more devastating effect 30 years later. And that is why history will remember Sean Cloney for much more than the humour and dignity with which he sustained the suffering of his last years. It will remember him as a beacon of enlightenment in a society still so riddled with superstition that, at the end of the 20th century, its more benighted members could regard that suffering as a punishment for his independence of spirit.

It will remember Sean Cloney, above all, as a role model whose resistance to clerical oppression, at a time when to resist the power of the priest was to risk widespread vilification and abuse, was little short of heroic.

In Fethard today the memory of Fortune remains strong; it causes division and there is still puzzlement and hurt when people speak of Bishop Comiskey. In the early 1990s, people in Fethard say, they were distressed at the retirement of Canon Willie Mernagh, by then in his eighties. They felt upset at this happening to a man who had been a simple, honest priest dedicated to the good of the parish for decades, who was happy to live out his days there. On retirement he moved out of the area to live with a relative in another part of the county and died a short time later. Another Wexford priest says it was very sad thing to see.

"Outsiders wonder why people in Fethard did nothing about Fortune, but we were looking to the people who we felt could do something. What could you do? People were afraid."

Kathleen, whose brother Jim was abused by Fortune and who was cursed by Fortune when she told him she did not want him to christen her baby girl, says the true horror of what went on in Fethard will never be known.

"There are lots of horror stories in this parish but people don't want to speak out. For every one that you hear about, there are several more. Then there are the people who would never hear a bad word against him right up until the end. Now, I think they just want it all to be forgotten about. I had mixed feelings about his suicide. On one hand I felt it was better to see him gone and able to do no more damage, but he was never proven guilty and that makes me mad. I wouldn't have cared what kind of sentence he would have got; I just wanted to hear the judge say that he was guilty.

"Nobody ever got up in the church here in Poulfur and said they were sorry for what went on. Maybe there are legal things that would stop them, but I don't see what that has to do with saying sorry. To this day nothing has ever been said to us."

Kathleen explains that she shudders now when she thinks of what went on in the house where Fortune lived and abused. The house remains, although Fr Joe McGrath, the parish priest, can no longer bear to live there. The offices are used during the day, but he prefers to leave it at night. He lives in a rented house and is hoping to build elsewhere in the parish. Too many horrible memories there, he told his parishioners. They respect Fr McGrath, and they understand his decision to move.

For their parts, Paul Molloy, Colm O'Gorman, Don and other victims certainly feel they have been failed. However, they are constrained in what they say by their impending civil actions. Two others are also suing and they may be joined by others in the future.

"I have absolutely no time for the man [Comiskey]. I feel he is a big coward," says Paul Molloy. He feels that while the bishop is entrusted with the well being of the people of the diocese, it did not seem to Paul himself this had been his primary consideration when dealing with Fortune. Paul is particularly perplexed and angry that Fortune was able to continue with radio and newspaper work after his complaint against him in 1988, and also that he was given another parish posting. "Of course there were complaints against him even before he was ordained. I have heard stories of him in St Peter's College. What went on is just unbelievable."

It is clear in conversation that Don, who had a strong Catholic influence from his parents, has mixed feelings about the bishop and his handling of Fortune.

"Yes, you can blame Brendan, but a lot of people knew what Johnny was up to but did nothing about it. You can blame the Scouts Association who took him on, and the Parents' Council of the Scouts group. You can blame the clerics. They hated the bastard and seemed to do nothing about him. You can blame the seminarians who knew about him and did nothing. You can blame the people who were told and did nothing. It is not that I don't blame the bishop but that he shared responsibility with these people. If the Church knew before he became a priest what he was up to, then that puts the whole thing in a very serious light. Apart from my faith, I have large amounts of resentment against the Church and the years of anger I went through. I know my dad feels huge guilt, but you cannot be there twenty-four hours a day. I also had to acknowledge that this was not my fault. I did things that I did not want to do. I let myself . . . but it was not my fault. I had to realise that."

Don's parents do not hold the bishop wholly responsible either, pointing to others who were told about Fortune's activities. "When the chips are down, I don't know whether he is a good man or a bad man, but I do know that he has great courage and great heart. People pulled him down for various reasons," says Michael.

His wife nods her head in agreement. "Everybody was waiting for him to be pulled down. I think he is more to be pitied than to be blamed. The people who were advising him did him no favours. Obviously I was involved in the whole thing for a long time, but it was only after his death that I realised the true extent of Fortune's sins, the evil he did and the disrepute he brought the Church into. A lot of people in authority in the Church were told about him, including Bishop Comiskey. Michael was fairly tenacious and kept on making complaints," she says.

It is clear in conversation with this loving couple that the abuse suffered by their son almost twenty years ago continues to cause grief and guilt. Brid mentions an interview she read with her son in the week following Fortune's suicide, where he told the story of what had happened to him.

"I was amazed that my little boy could have had all that in his heart and in his head for so many years – while he was in school, in college, out with his friends, through his marriage. I thought he had gotten over it. There was no outward sign of it, but I now realise that he had not forgotten one word, or one look. It was all festering there for so long. It was as if it had happened yesterday. That really upset me. I could sit down and cry. Like all parents we were very careful and when the boys were little before they went anywhere they would chant back at me, as I was about to give them the familiar warning, 'We know, don't speak to strange men in toilets.' I had heard some rumours about Fortune, but it was a different time then and it just seemed incredible. Don had gone to Poulfur before, but he was with his brother and I believed that they were safe together. But then Fortune came and took him away, on his own, when we were away. It was a terrible thing that he did."

Both Don and Colm O'Gorman have strong feelings about the manner in which society treats the problem of paedophilia. Colm is one of the founders of a charity in the UK which helps people who have been sexually abused. The charity's name, One in Four, he explains, refers to the number of people who it is estimated will be sexually abused by the time they are eighteen. It is run for and by people who have been abused.

"People say he [Fortune] was a monster and needed to be locked up, but he was a human being as well, and there are reasons why he did what he did. Child abuse is the responsibility of everyone, not just the victims or the perpetrators. It is the responsibility of society. When he was born he was just a baby and then a little boy. He wasn't evil. He wasn't a monster; he became one with his behaviour, and there is no point in just demonising him. He lost his humanity, but he was helped along the way by people who deliberately did things to him. From what I heard about his background there were a lot of problems. Having said that, he was responsible for what he did. I absolutely see that his behaviour was evil, monstrous and demonic, but he was a human being, and I do not believe he was inherently evil. I reject what he became, but if he is simply demonised society is left off the hook."

Colm says that what he is seeking from the Catholic Church is an acknowledgement of what occurred; a full disclosure of what they knew and how they acted; what they knew about Fortune's behaviour before he was ordained.

"Someone as damaged as him should clearly not have been put in authority. He was completely out of control. The man was dangerous and in a dangerous place emotionally. The Church was not. The Church is a great and powerful institution. It has authority. Sean Fortune's behaviour may be explained by trauma, psychological problems, mental illness. What is the Church's excuse? I don't know what any individual within the Church knew, and if they didn't, why not? It was very obvious what was going on. I would like a frank disclosure of the truth."

If he were to communicate a message to others who have been sexually abused, it would be this: "It is not a life sentence. You can never change it, you can't make it something good, but you do have to face it head on, go right into the horror of it. You can get beyond it and get back to being a human being. There is more to you than the fact that you were raped as a child, or the fear that people you have spoken to about it will look at you and want to throw up. All my life I used to believe that I was evil, not just bad but evil. But that has changed."

Don has spent considerable time studying paedophilia and its possible causes. Its depiction as something carried out by "sex beasts" annoys him.

"There is a witch hunt out there, but witch hunts do nothing to help these people. My friends hate when I go on about this, but we have to look at it. People tend to think that the lines between sexuality are very well defined but, in fact, they are vague. Everyone has their own fetishes and foibles. If you are that way inclined towards kiddies, whether it is genetic or as a result of experience – nature or nurture – the view at the moment is that it is a combination of both factors. But if people do get into a situation where they do abuse someone, then there is nothing that society does to help them to address it. Even if they feel they have those tendencies, there is nowhere for them to go. You are not going to cure paedophiles, you must keep them away from children, but you can help them. If you have your own children, for the first time in a long time you are looking at genitals in a non-sexual way. Parents do have a tiny portion of attraction towards their children and that is normal, as long as it does not get out of hand. On television if you see a naked woman's bum you go 'Wow'; if you see something similar but smaller there is that nanosecond . . . but then you pass on, you see that it is a child. I can make a distinction but many people feel guilty about it. Let's face it, Ireland is a case study in guilt and repression.

"If there is a debate on television about paedophilia, it is never a constructive one. Demonising of paedophiles – who does that satisfy, only people with an insatiable desire for gore. If I were a paedophile, I would be waiting for someone to go on television and say, 'It's all right, we can discuss this.' Imagine if you were someone who started having these kind of feelings; you would be scared to mention it to anybody and then it gets too late."

Asked if these thoughts on paedophilia extended to his own abuser, Don pauses. "Fortune, if he had not killed himself, should have been locked away. Any psychiatric evaluation would have found him a hopeless case. If he did go on a treatment course, though, he would have been engaging, smiling, taking part. The best trained psychiatrist in the world would have thought he was progressing. He had stuff happening on so many other levels apart from just child abuse."

Don explains his motive for going ahead with a civil case.

"I expected at the end of the case that the Church would come out and apologise, but they just shut up shop, even though others have done it. When it comes down to the everyday common sense things, the bishop [Comiskey] is fine. He has strong faith and a strong knowledge of faith, but if you are going to be teaching love and understanding, the least you can do is practise what you preach. I am bringing the Church to court but I am not out for revenge. They have not apologised. If what happened to me never happens to anyone else, that is fine, but they didn't apologise and they have to be made responsible." Don's family and the other families still find themselves unable to move on as they wait for the outcome of these civil cases.

In August, over five months after his death, the priest's inquest was held in New Ross. Like everything else to do with Fortune, it had its unusual moments. There was the customary gathering in the town's courthouse of gardaí, doctors, journalists and the Wexford county coroner, James Murphy. Seated in the public gallery was Fr Joe McGrath, parish priest of Fethard-on-Sea, and behind him Eileen Molloy, Paul's mother. Both were obviously linked to Fortune but it seemed odd that they would be there. As it turned out, their presence was coincidental. They were there for an inquest into the death in a fire of an elderly Fethard man for whom Eileen Molloy had acted as home help. Arriving at the house after the fire had broken out, she made valiant efforts to drag the man outside but tragically he died. After she and Fr McGrath gave evidence in that case, they remained to listen as the Fortune inquest got underway.

In the cramped press gallery the journalists began writing furiously as the story of his suicide unfolded. Margaret Stamp, his devoted housekeeper of fourteen years, and caretaker Peter Bennett told of Fortune's instructions to them and of their finding him dead. Peter told the inquest that he had never seen the priest drink alcohol before, although he saw an empty whiskey bottle in the room that morning. In the three years that he had known the priest, he never talked about the allegations against him, said the caretaker, but then he added that the priest had always protested his innocence. A local garda told the inquest that their inquiries ascertained that the last known contact Fortune had with anyone was with Margaret and Peter on the telephone the previous Thursday night.

Dr Joseph O'Connor, who carried out the post-mortem, said the death was due to central cardio-respiratory failure due to a multiple overdose of drugs and alcohol. The drugs used had been prescribed to Fortune for nerves, stress and pain. Death, Dr O'Connor estimated, had taken place thirty-six hours or longer before he had been found on Saturday morning.

Afterwards the coroner extended his sympathy to the Fortune family, none of whom were present that morning. Nor did there appear to be any official representative of the Diocese of Ferns.

According to the other detail contained in the will, Fortune left his personal effects, including books and a silver chalice, to his family. His housekeeper, Margaret Stamp, was named as the beneficiary of two named bank accounts. The remainder of his estate, he said, was to go to his siblings. The will has not yet been published.

Fortune's death brought no further clarity to his financial affairs. One way of discovering what happened to all of his money could be to follow a trail of the money coming in and out of the two accounts.

The Fortune family decided against taking part in this book, feeling that it was too soon. Theirs is an unenviable position, torn between reconciling the love of a brother, whom they believe was abused himself, and the desperate deeds that were alleged against him which caused so much hurt. They knew he could be a bully, but there was another side of him which could be very caring, and he would always help out if he could. After his funeral they received letters from some people telling them how helpful he had been to them.

They wonder why he was sent to Mountjoy when psychiatric treatment was ordered. What was it that pushed him over the edge on that night he committed suicide? Why did the Church not take steps to protect their brother from himself and to protect others, particularly if they were told he had problems? Did anyone investigate the abuse he said he suffered as a child and during his teenage years? Why was he named in the newspapers and not other priests accused of child abuse? He told them he was being blackmailed and lived in fear of his life. The security shutters placed on the house were not the actions of a lunatic but of a man who was terrified, they believed. In his suicide letter he said he wanted one of his brothers to have his collection of newspaper articles concerning his case; when added together they apparently came to thirty-eight broadsheet pages. When his brother finally felt able to go through the papers, he saw among them the medical reports and psychiatric assessments going back a number of years. It seemed they had been left there specifically for him to find, to provide some answers. It struck the family how long the Church had known their brother had problems.

Despite a number of requests, Dr Comiskey declined to be interviewed for this book. It was suggested, through his spokeswoman, that he might answer faxed questions. In the event, he declined to give any answers to those either. The only response was the forwarding of a copy of a letter sent to him on 2 November 1999 from diocesan solicitor Paul Ebrill of Kirwan & Kirwan Solicitors.

> I have studied the correspondence sent by the above journalist to Barbara Wallace seeking an interview and in lieu thereof requesting a response to a series of questions raised by her.
>
> A substantial number of the questions asked recite, within the questions themselves, contentions couched as facts upon which contentious elements of the book are likely to be based. If such is to be the case then I would hope that the journalist would proceed cautiously in accepting as fact many unsubstantiated accounts of events and merely because they have been recounted in the media.
>
> Furthermore there is the legal issue arising from the fact that there is litigation in train and also threatened against your Diocese arising out of alleged conduct on the part of Fr Sean Fortune during his lifetime. You personally as the Bishop of the Diocese are cited as a Defendant in these proceedings and may further be cited as a Defendant in proceedings yet to be instituted.
>
> For both of the foregoing reasons I would advise you against replying to the questions asked by this journalist.
>
> There does not appear to me to be any benefit to any party, other than those who may profit from the publication, which would indicate that your co-operation with this publication would be advisable.

And so the sorry saga continues with the civil actions.

Paul Molloy's case has been the first to go ahead and it is being fought every step of the way. The other defendants, apart from Dr Comiskey, are the papal nuncio and Fortune, whose estate remains part of the case despite his death. It is thought to be the first attempt to make the Church in Rome liable for alleged abuse in Ireland. Paul's case claims that Bishop Comiskey and the nuncio were negligent and in breach of their duty to him and others in admitting Fortune to ordination and to a ministry in which he had power and dominion over children and unsupervised contact with them.

He is seeking a declaration that, having embarked on an inquiry into the sexual assaults suffered by himself, there was a duty to complete the inquiry or to notify the defendant of their intention not to complete the inquiry. He claims that they acted in breach of their duty to inform his parents that there were reasonable grounds for assuming that he had been sexually abused by Fr Fortune and that they were not going to complete an inquiry into that fact. He is also seeking damages for personal injury and assault. These claims are being denied by Bishop Comiskey, while the nuncio is claiming entitlement to diplomatic immunity.

Of course it is another long wait for him and the others, but there is the hope that, finally, there may be recognition from the legal system of their suffering and the hope, perhaps in vain, that the Church, albeit forced to do so, will offer the same recognition.

SOME OTHER READING
from
BRANDON

SEAN O'CALLAGHAN

To Hell or Barbados
The ethnic cleansing of Ireland

Between 1652 and 1659 over 50,000 Irish men, women and children were transported to Barbados and Virginia. Yet until now there has been no account of what became of them.

The motivation for the initial transportation of the Irish was expressed by King James I of England: "Root out the Papists and fill it [Ireland] with Protestants."

The author's search began in the library of the Barbados Museum and Historical Society and its files on Irish slaves. Sean O'Callaghan for the first time documents the history of these people: their transportation, the conditions in which they lived on plantations as slaves or servants, and their rebellions in Barbados.

Sean O'Callaghan is the author of fourteen previous books, including *The Slave Trade in Africa*, which was translated into thirteen languages and filmed by Malenotti of Rome.

ISBN 0 86322 272 2; Hardback £15.99

EAMONN McCANN

Bloody Sunday in Derry
What Really Happened

On 30th January 1972 the Parachute Regiment shot twenty-seven unarmed civil rights demonstrators in Derry. Fourteen men and boys died on what has come to be known as Bloody Sunday.

At the heart of the book are fourteen pieces about those who died. Each is an account by a relative, friend, neighbour or other associate of the dead person. There is also a compelling account of the events of that day and their aftermath, and a detailed analysis of the Widgery Report, which, it concludes, was the single greatest travesty of justice arising out of the Northern Ireland turmoil of the past three decades.

"This moving and impressive book is cumulatively powerful. The *tour de force* of the book is its description of Lord Widgery's Tribunal. As a mendacious and arrogant piece of judicial trumpery, it can hardly be equalled." *Guardian*

"Nobody should moralise about the Northern Troubles without reading it." *Phoenix*

"A highly successful formula of 'unsanitised' primary sources, oral history and political commentary and analysis. The layout of the book makes for easy reading of a complex and disturbing truth." *Books Ireland*

ISBN 0 86322 274 9; Paperback £9.99

JOHN TROLAN

Slow Punctures

"Compelling. . . his writing, with its mix of brutal social realism, irony and humour, reads like a cross between Roddy Doyle and Irvine Welsh." *Sunday Independent*

"Three hundred manic, readable pages. . . *Slow Punctures* is grim, funny and bawdy in equal measure." *The Irish Times*

"Fast-moving and hilarious in the tradition of Roddy Doyle." *Sunday Business Post*

"Trolan writes in a crisp and consistent style. He handles the delicate subject of young suicide with a sensitive practicality and complete lack of sentiment. His novel is a brittle working-class rites of passage that tells a story about Dublin that probably should have been told a long time ago." *Irish Post*

ISBN 0 86322 252 8; Original Paperback £8.99

Any Other Time

"Trolan's portrayal of a hopeless underclass is both convincing and chilling . . . He has a rare and genuine gift for dialogue, and his characters' voices ring true. A relentlessly grim but undeniably powerful novel." *Sunday Tribune*

"Wonderfully written, and confirms Trolan's talent . . . Such is the power of Trolan's writing, and so skilful his descriptions and characterisation, that before long I was mesmerised by the seedy world I had landed in . . . Trolan writes from the inside, and it show." *Books Ireland*

John Trolan was born in a Dublin tenement in 1960, and lived for fifteen years in the high-rise flats of Ballymun. After a period of homelessness he studied at university in Bristol and took a degree. He now works as an addictions counsellor in Stroud and is actively involved in the performance poetry scene in Bristol.

ISBN 0 86322 265 X; Original Paperback £8.99

GERRY ADAMS

An Irish Voice
The Quest for Peace

with an introduction by Niall O'Dowd

"The importance of this collection from one of the foremost revolutionary figures of the late 20th century becomes immediately evident . . . And, as these articles show, he is a thinker of considerable stature . . . *An Irish Voice* is a good read. For the humour as much as the philosophy or the politics." Tim Pat Coogan, *The Irish Times*

ISBN 1 902011 01 5; Paperback £9.99

STEVE MACDONOGH
Open Book: One Publisher's War

"MacDonogh is without doubt the most adventurous and determined of the Irish publishers . . . This is an important book." *Phoenix*

"A fascinating and very important book." Brid Rosney, Today FM

"The parallels between Orwell and MacDonogh are striking . . . MacDonogh's transparent writing is redolent of Orwell's famous 'plain style'. Most significant of all, . . . Orwell believed that the fate of democracy is linked with that of literature. MacDonogh's career is an illustration of that point . . . *Open Book* is an intelligent, informative account of a life spent fighting for freedom of speech, a right which is still not adequately safeguarded."
Irish World

"Fascinating reading." *Sunday Business Post*

ISBN 0 86322 263 3; Paperback £8.99